DATE	

Montessori

Prescription for Children
with Learning Disabilities

Montessori

Prescription for Children with Learning Disabilities

R. C. Orem &
Marjorie Foster Coburn

Capricorn Books
G. P. Putnam's Sons
New York

Acknowledgments

Thanks go to—
The children who have found they can learn and be successful. Their joy in their own accomplishments is a special gift.

The parents who have been through many mazes in the process of recognition, diagnosis, and placement.

Albert D. Leary, Jr., executive director of Leary School, who had the courage to try Montessori at his school and gave Marjorie Foster Coburn the right amount of freedom and support.

Carol Sears, learning disabilities specialist, who confirmed the suspicion that Montessori is applicable to the needs of the learning-disabled child.

The staff of the Montessori Primary Unit: Janet Fairbank, Millie Ulrich, Henry Ticknor, Margaret Conley, Barbara Tiplady, Sue Bickel, Barbi Leary, Kevin Rehrig, Sue Davy, Janet Sheffield, and Jesse Spurway.

The support staff of Leary School, who were especially helpful: Dr. Sandra Rubin, Betsy Anderson, Mary Alice Venuto, Anne Hyland, Robert Iarrobino, Elsie Selman, Betty Brodes, Su Coursey, Virginia Schaufelberger, and Sue Burke-Ticknor.

The contributors of this book: Mary Alice Venuto, Betsy Anderson, Janet Fairbank, Anne Hyland, Ann O'Keefe, and two parents who wrote their own children's stories.

The photographer: Robert Iarrobino.

And Nancy Simmons and Barbara Newman, who typed it all.

For Polly and Matt Foster,
who introduced me both to children and to Montessori
MARJORIE FOSTER COBURN

And for Robbie Earley
R. C. OREM

Preface

Montessori: Prescription for Children with Learning Disabilities will be welcomed by parents as well as by professional educators. The book not only draws on Maria Montessori's philosophy, principles, materials, and methods and relates them to the needs of children with learning disabilities, but also draws upon the experience and hard-won wisdom of parents themselves—parents who have had to confront the problems of learning disabilities, who have faced with their own children the frustrations of such disabilities, and who have found some answers to their dilemmas.

As national director of the Office of Child Development's Home Start Program since its beginning in 1971, I have been especially interested in the kinds of resources and guidance that are available to parents as they fulfill their role as the earliest and most influential educators of their own children. Home Start was developed as an additional approach within Head Start to help parents provide for their own children, in their own homes, many of the same kinds of experiences provided for children in Head Start child-development centers. Although Home Start programs were funded for low-income families (since by law Head Start is primarily a program intended for low-income families), the Home Start concept has been

9

well-received—often eagerly received—and widely utilized by parents at all income levels.

This new book, weaving together as it does the work of Montessori, present-day professional educators, and parents seasoned by their struggles with learning disabilities in their own children, is a practical resource fully in tune with current trends, which emphasize providing educational opportunities for all, individualizing programs to meet children's needs while building upon their strengths, and capitalizing on the role of parents as partners in the educational development of their own children.

—RUTH ANN O'KEEFE, ED.D.
Director, Home Start
and Child and Family
Resource Program

Contents

11

Foreword

How the Montessori Method Can Help the Learning-Disabled Child

The Montessori program has proved very helpful for children with certain types of learning disabilities. Both the materials and the methods have been used diagnostically and remedially in self-contained preschool and primary programs, with teenagers in a special tutorial program, and as supplements to the learning-disabilities program at the intermediate and junior-high levels.

Many workers in the field of learning disabilities are now moving in the direction of a "task-analytic" approach, but Maria Montessori was using this approach as early as the nineteenth century. In her method, appropriate tasks are carefully chosen and presented in sequential order to each child individually. Because Montessori believed in not asking more from a child than he was able to give, she sequenced her materials in accordance with developmental principles.

The presentation of the tasks begins with breaking each one down into the various subskills necessary to assure success. They are introduced with a minimum of speech and a maximum of demonstration by the teacher. Thus the teacher serves first as a demonstrator presenting the stimuli, which are attractive materials designed for maximum contrast. Next she becomes an observer, noting the child's problem-solving processes. Finally, the Montessori method is adjusted to allow for alternative ways of presenting the task based upon the child's strengths and weaknesses. All the tasks have a built-in "control of error" so that the child can gain immediate feedback as he works to solve the task confronting him. Thus he learns by doing, rather than by being subjected to constant correction by the teacher.

Another aspect of the Montessori method that helps the learning-disabled child is its structure. The classroom with its "prepared environment" contributes tremendously to the structure so needed by the child with learning disabilities. For example, furniture is scaled to the size of the child, so that he is better able to coordinate himself and use the facilities of the room. Everything has a proper place and a definite purpose. Though there is freedom of movement within the Montessori classroom, this freedom comes with certain limits on behavior. Each child may choose an area of personal space, which may be a table or a mat on the floor. No other child may enter this work space unless he has been invited by the child who has claimed the space. No scheduled bells interrupt the child as he concentrates on mastering a task. He is never hurried, and he is allowed to repeat the task as many times as necessary for him to feel successful.

Marjorie Foster Coburn has made significant modifications in the Montessori environment in order to accommodate the learning-disabled child: smaller class size and classrooms, for example, and displaying the Montessori equipment in such a way as to minimize distractions. These and other modifications have helped the learning-disabled child obtain the focus necessary for effective learning.

The Montessori curriculum begins with one of the earliest things learned—movement. The motor (movement) education program includes care of the self and the environment, exercises to promote the development of the gross (large) muscles of the body and the fine (small) muscles of the hand, and work on body image and awareness. This includes measuring oneself, balancing and walking on a line drawn on the floor, trampoline work, calisthenics, movement through an obstacle course and on the "Stegel," which is a multilevel apparatus designed to facilitate large-muscle development.

The freedom of movement within the Montessori classroom encourages the normal bodily movements such as walking, standing, kneeling, and sitting. Some movements are put to rhythm in order to promote awareness of time passing and to foster the development of doing a task in a step-by-step manner in a logical sequence. Children walk on the line with books on their heads or flowers in their hands, with eyes straight ahead. They practice hopping, skipping, and marching to rhythm. The practical life exercises foster the development of the fine motor abilities, particularly the eye-hand coordination skills necessary for coping with daily life. These include pouring one's own juice, washing tables, polishing metals, polishing one's shoes, buttoning, snapping, lacing, and clipping clothespins to hang up wet dishcloths. The task presentation is usually in a consistent left-to-right orientation, so that as the child moves about the Montessori classroom and performs the various tasks, he is stabilizing his awareness of the sides of the body (laterality) and the directions in which it moves (directionality). At the same time, the student develops appropriate social skills and independence, which enhance the learning-disabled child's self-concept.

The concrete sensorial materials, which provide multisensory and/or unisensory experiences, have helped the perceptually impaired make order out of their chaotic perceptual world. The experiences isolate a single attribute upon which the child focuses through seeing, hearing, touching, lifting, pushing, pulling, smelling, or tasting. As the child practices discrimination, noting differences in such things as color, sound, texture, weight, and temperature, he begins eventually to compare and classify, to move from the concrete to the abstract. All this culminates in concept development and thinking abilities.

As the child proceeds along the continuum in the curriculum set up for the refinement of perceptual abilities, he will begin to develop language abilities. For example, while the child is building the pink tower, an activity designed to develop visual perception (in this case, size discrimination), he will be learning quantitative terms such as *large, larger, largest, small, smaller, smallest*. While working with the brown stair materials, he will be grading them according to thickness and learning the terms *thick, thicker, thickest, thin, thinner, thinnest*. Children learn the names of geometric forms through matching and tracing the plane geometric forms in the geometric cabinet, an exercise in form perception. They learn the names of all the continents and countries in the world while putting pieces into a puzzle-map of the continents. The chromatic scale is introduced, and in addition to developing color perception, the child grades the various shades and learns such terminology as *light, lighter, lightest,* and *dark, darker, darkest.*

While matching sounds made by boxes containing materials that make various soft and loud noises and then grading them from soft to loud, the child learns the comparative adjectives describing the sounds he hears. There are exercises in which the child identifies voices with his eyes closed, trying to determine which classmate is speaking. There is training in auditory sequential memory, through learning the days of the week and the months of the year and learning the temporal concepts of yesterday, today, and tomorrow. A typical auditory figure-ground experience includes exercises wherein the child demonstrates and names an instrument that he hears in a symphony as it stands out against a background of the orchestra. Thus the child is continually being asked to focus on pertinent auditory stimuli, whether it be through listening games or through matching or grading sounds.

The development of the stereognostic sense—identifying a shape by feeling with the hands—is, of course, primary in the Montessori method. Much of the learning takes place using this in combination with the other senses. We see this tactile-kinesthetic (touching-moving) perceptual development in such activities as identification of various fabrics and work with the knobbed cylinders (which develops the pincer grasp), the geometric solids, and rough and smooth boards.

These practical life and perceptual activities are meant to serve as precursors to reading, writing, and mathematics development. They provide the child with verbal and nonverbal experiences that help him understand concepts and prepare him in skills that are critical to successful performance in the three major academic areas.

The formal academic materials that require reading and writing are introduced when the child shows he is ready for them and has made sufficient progress toward remediating perceptual or other deficiencies that would otherwise impede his performance.

The child with reading disabilities (dyslexia) may profit from the Montessori reading approach, a multisensory approach whereby the child first matches the sound of a letter to a corresponding sandpaper letter. He progresses to using the three-dimensional letters of the movable alphabet, which he uses to spell words dictated by the teacher or suggested by picture cards.

Practice with tracing sandpaper letters and with the movable alphabet, together with cutting with scissors and tracing metal insets, prepares the child for formal writing lessons. Initially the child practices writing the alphabet and copying words. Eventually, he progresses to writing his own stories. The Montessori method is modified for the child having extreme difficulty with writing (dysgraphia), breaking the letters down into strokes and stressing the order in which they are written. In addition, special red-lined paper is used to help the child focus on the spaces and lines in which to write.

Disabilities in mathematics may result from both verbal and nonverbal deficiencies: in reading word problems and understanding quantitative language on the one hand; in visual-spatial functioning and inability to grasp cognitive principles such as the conservation of quantity on the other hand. Practical life exercises such as measuring solids and pouring liquids, together with perceptual activities developing awareness of size, form, and sequence prepare the child with a math disability to cope with the concepts of formal mathematics by providing him with direct experiences that allow him to symbolize quantitative relationships.

The Montessori math equipment, which consists of concrete manipulable objects, has proved very useful, even with teenagers who have had trouble grasping mathematical concepts all their lives. There are many counting exercises that involve matching objects to numerals, and the child learns to count with beads by twos, by threes, by fours, and so on. These exercises lead the child to visualize groups. The bank game, which introduces the decimal system, is a learning game that also teaches the child place value and introduces addition, subtraction, multiplication, and division. Extensions of the bank game lead the child to abstraction and memorization of mathematical facts. All these activities are carefully sequenced so that the concrete materials will lead eventually to mastery of the four major arithmetic operations and will also prepare the child for higher mathematics.

These are but a few of the Montessori methods and materials that have been used successfully to remediate learning disabilities. Many more are elaborated upon in this unique and helpful book.

—MARY ALICE VENUTO, M.A., C.A.G.S.
Learning Disabilities Specialist

Introduction

Leary School was founded in 1964 for students who needed a small classroom, individual attention, and careful guidance in order to reach their academic potential. The school is located in Falls Church, Virginia, and draws students from Virginia, Maryland, and the District of Columbia. The 160 students have learning disabilities, emotional problems, or both. The character of the student body has changed in recent years due to changes in federal and school-district funding, so that now the students tend to be more severely handicapped at admission than formerly.

The Montessori method came to Leary School on an experimental basis in September 1970. This was after almost a year of discussion between Albert D. Leary, Jr., founder and executive director of Leary School, and Marjorie Foster Coburn, a social worker and Association Montessori Internationale–trained Montessori teacher.

They wondered whether the theory and techniques Montessori designed for use with three- to six-year-old children might help students of seven to sixteen who have learning and emotional problems. They believed that work with the Montessori manipulable academic materials would aid students who had been unable to learn from traditional textbook, blackboard, and lecture techniques.

For the first two years, the Leary Montessori program served as a

19

backup technique for students aged seven to sixteen who needed even more help than they were receiving in their small classes. These students were referred to the Montessori Resource Room. The room had one large table in the center and was lined with dark-stained shelves containing three areas of the Montessori curriculum: sensorial, language, and mathematics. Also included were other manipulable materials, such as inch cubes and parquetry. The room was clean, attractive, and looked as though it were meant for adults, not children. The students came individually or in small groups. None of them seemed to realize that the equipment had been designed for preschool children—it was challenging and appealed to them.

When a student was referred, the teacher would bring him to the room alone, where they discussed the reason for referral. The student was asked about his view of his academic needs. (The children proved to be surprisingly candid.) Then she showed him the materials that might be of use to him and demonstrated a piece of equipment just below what she thought was his success level. As the student did the task, she was able to observe how he functioned and to decide at which step of the Montessori curriculum to place him. Each student was assigned to a small group of approximately his own age.

The half-hour sessions once or twice a week looked like a normal small Montessori class, except that the children were older than usual. A group of eight- and nine-year-olds might be working on the trinomial cube, the addition strip board, and the sandpaper letters. Later in the day, a group of teenagers might be working on the same tasks. The age of the children did not seem to matter. What mattered was their need to work with their hands and their own sensitivity to their academic needs.

After two years, the following observations were made:

1. The older learning-disabled child who has not been able to perceive his environment correctly shares some of the needs of the preschool child who has not matured enough to perceive correctly.

2. The Montessori equipment is an excellent learning aid because it allows the child to learn with all his senses and through his own activity.

3. Older children are as sensitive to their own needs as preschool children. For instance, students who need work in math freely chose

to work at math. Those still in need of size discrimination chose work in that area. Allowed to work at their own pace and with repetition, they become more confident.

4. Behavior problems rarely existed in the Montessori Resource Room. Occasionally a student would enter upset but would grow calm as he worked quietly with his hands. There was no need for formal behavior modification. Success led to happiness.

At the end of two years, Albert Leary and Marjorie Foster Coburn believed that the Montessori theory, techniques, and equipment were indeed applicable to the learning-disabled child. They decided to apply it full-time to the youngest children in the school.

In 1972, the Montessori Primary Unit was started with two classes, one for children from six to eight years of age who had few academic skills, and one for seven- to nine-year-olds who had rudimentary academic skills.

The Montessori environment was simplified and adapted to the children. Most of them were hyperactive. All were learning disabled. Some had emotional problems. Learning from their own observations, the staff added to the curriculum. They used the principles of Montessori. The children were treated with great respect. Lessons were individualized. Movement, quiet conversation, and some freedom of choice of work was permitted. When they were ready, the children were introduced to traditional materials such as texts and workbooks. The Gillingham program to teach reading and writing using the sounds of letters proved to be an effective extension of the Montessori work with sandpaper letters and movable alphabet.

The staff grew in understanding as the children grew. When the parents came to observe, they could not believe how much their children were learning and how well behaved they were. Many teachers and educators came and asked how they could adapt these techniques to their own programs. They had difficulty believing the children had severe learning problems since they were working so well and appeared happy and well behaved.

The Montessori unit has expanded to include several more classes. A transitional class was developed for children who have some academic skills but still need Montessori materials to help explain a concept or develop a skill, and other transitional classes based on this class have been added. The Montessori classes are taught by Montessori teachers who also use special-education techniques. The transitional classes are taught by special-education teachers who use Montessori techniques. The techniques blend beautifully.

The support staff of Leary School is available to the teachers and provides essential services to the children. The speech therapist sees over half the children. A psychologist does play therapy and testing. She also consults with the teachers and parents. The learning-disability specialist is available for consultation and program planning with the teachers. The art teacher works with the children once a week, giving lessons designed to increase their learning abilities.

If the teachers had to choose three key words to describe the basis of their success, the words would be *structure, individualization,* and *success.*

Teachers *structure* the environment—gear it to the child's size and needs. They structure the lessons for success, and structure the rules of conduct to encourage acceptable behavior.

Individualization comes through observation and knowing as much as possible about each child before he enters the school. Most knowledge about the child comes from careful observation of him, learning his strengths and weaknesses and planning a program for him that builds on the strengths and diminishes the weaknesses. Lessons are usually individual. Few children are at the same place in the curriculum at the same time.

Success is the key to a happy, learning child. Having small successes grows into a feeling of competence and being worthwhile. As the child grows in confidence, his academic accomplishments and self-concept increase.

A few words of caution. Montessori dovetails with learning-disability theory, but a regular Montessori classroom will still have too much movement, too many people and things for a distractible youngster. The learning-disabled child needs a quieter, more protected environment.

The Montessori teacher of the learning-disabled child must have both experience with ordinary children and training in teaching children with learning disabilities, either through a university or through an in-service program. Ideally, the teacher has the support of other professionals, such as psychologists, motor-development specialists, speech pathologists, and educational diagnosticians. In short, the Montessori environment, theory, techniques, and materials are quite applicable to children with learning disabilities, but must be adapted for these children.

SECTION ONE

Montessori

1. Montessori: Questions and Answers*

Who was Dr. Montessori?
  Maria Montessori was an Italian medical doctor (1870–1952) who became interested in how children learn and developed a system to encourage them to learn. Her theories appear to be applicable to almost every child. (See the following Biographical Sketch for more details about this remarkable woman.)

What is the Montessori method?
  An educational approach, including defined principles and practices, named for the founder. Basically, this method employs great respect for the child and his development. An environment is carefully prepared for his exploration, and his self-development is encouraged.

What is the basic principle of the Montessori method?
  The liberty of the student, enabling him to achieve self-discipline through his own activity. The purpose is to prepare the child for life.

  *The authors conduct Montessori seminars at which certain questions regarding Maria Montessori, her method, and the Montessori movement tend to recur.
  Brief answers to a compilation of the most frequently asked questions are given here.

What does the method consist of?
The core of the method is a sequence of activities and materials designed to enable the child to teach himself. The classroom structure encourages each child to make choices and to be free to learn and respect himself and others.

How can the child teach himself?
The Montessori materials have a built-in "control of error," which provides the learner with information as to the accuracy of his response and enables him to correct himself. The teacher demonstrates the exercise initially and is available if needed. Often the children teach each other. Through repetition, the child masters each exercise and becomes ready to move on to the next one.

Does the Montessori method restrict the child's creativity?
Montessori's whole approach is based upon recognition of the child's creativity and his need for an environment that encourages rather than limits this creativity.
The child is given the opportunity to master the tools of creativity, which allows for a higher plane of expression.

Is the method for young children only?
No. Although Montessori did much of her work with preschoolers, her method is widely used at the elementary level also and, to a certain extent, beyond.

Is the method for certain categories of children only?
No. Use of the method is not restricted to any particular types or groups of children. It is employed with gifted, learning-disabled, normal, and retarded children. Since the children are encouraged to move through the curriculum at their own rates, each child can learn according to his own interests and capabilities.

How long has Montessori education been around?
Montessori opened her first school, Casa dei Bambini ("House of Children"), in Italy in 1907. The first Montessori school in America was opened in 1912, and her *Montessori Method*, published the same year, was a best-seller. But the widespread interest soon faded because the method was misused, and it was not until 1958 that the first

of the new wave of Montessori schools was founded in this country. The American Montessori Society was organized in 1960. The Association Montessori Internationale became active again in this country in 1960.

How many Montessori schools are there in the United States today?
It is estimated that there are nearly two thousand Montessori-oriented schools, ranging from one-room operations to elaborate facilities. Many of the schools are clustered in a relatively few metropolitan areas.

How expensive is Montessori education?
Costs vary widely. The longer the school day and the higher the grade level, the greater the cost. Some schools also provide transportation and other features.

How much freedom is allowed in the Montessori classroom?
There is "liberty within limits." A number of ground rules help preserve the order of the classroom as the students move about. For example, a child is not allowed to interfere with another child or that child's work, but he is allowed to choose where he would like to work, with what, and for how long. He also may choose to work alone or with others.

Do Montessori teachers ever have discipline problems?
Certainly. These problems are handled by the teacher giving the child more attention and getting him interested in some piece of apparatus in the classroom.
Children who are extremely hyperactive, insecure, or disturbed may need additional evaluation by a physician or psychologist.

How can I tell if a Montessori school is a good one?
Check it out. Visit and observe the classes after doing some reading on Montessori. Note the facilities, the program, the staff qualifications. Most important, note if the children are happy, if they are learning, and if you feel happy being there.

Is the name Montessori an assurance of quality?
No. Schools bearing the name Montessori vary enormously in

quality. Since the name Montessori is not controlled, many schools use it to capitalize on the interest in Montessori. It is important to check the credentials of the teachers and the school before enrolling your child. A good place to check is your nearest Montessori teacher-training institute. In order to obtain a complete list of Montessori-teacher-training institutes, write to both the American Montessori Society, 150 Fifth Avenue, New York, N. Y. 10011, and the Association Montessori Internationale, 2119 S Street N.W., Washington, D.C. 20008.

What is the basic difference between the Montessori environment and the traditional classroom?

In the Montessori classroom, there is often an age range of three years, there is freedom of movement, and the children work directly with Montessori materials of their own choosing individually or in small groups most of the time, rather than being dependent upon a teacher's directions.

In the traditional classroom, children of one age group spend most of their time sitting and watching an adult teach and impart knowledge. The lessons are typically group oriented, and the children are evaluated on their written work.

Do children have trouble adjusting to public school after Montessori?

Experience of the past fifteen years indicates that Montessori children are able to cope with the conditions they encounter when transferring to the public-school classroom. A better question would be: Are the public schools able to adjust to the needs of the Montessori-trained children for self-development?

Most public-school teachers report that their Montessori children are relatively independent, curious, have good work habits, and are generally quite kind to others. In general, they adjust to the public-school classroom well but do best in those classes which encourage discovery and individual rates of learning.

How does the Montessori teacher's role differ from that of the traditional teacher?

The Montessori teacher, or directress, as she is often called, gives individual and group lessons but spends much of her time observing each child, preparing his environment, and protecting his self-development.

The traditional teacher usually gives class lessons and gives the students assignments, which she later grades.

In the Montessori classroom, the children are actively involved in their learning while the teacher observes their needs and moves about the classroom giving lessons accordingly. In the traditional classroom, the children receive the lessons passively as they sit quietly in their seats. The teacher is the center of attention and giver of knowledge.

Is the Montessori approach utilized in regular public-school classrooms?

Basically not, but a handful of school districts are applying Montessori to some degree.

Although Maria Montessori is usually not given credit for many approaches currently being utilized in some public schools, many of the innovative ideas in education today were employed by her. Examples of this are multiage grouping, use of self-correcting and manipulable materials, students tutoring students, ungraded schools, parental observation and conferences, and individualized teaching.

Some school districts have included Montessori classes as a part of the regular program. This is an encouraging trend.

What is the admissions policy of Montessori schools regarding learning disabled and other special children?

There is no uniform policy. Some schools will enroll one or two children with diagnosed problems per class. There are some Montessori programs exclusively for children with developmental deficiencies and others that enroll no such children.

Did Montessori work with so-called culturally disadvantaged children?

Yes. As a matter of fact, her first school was opened in a tenement in the San Lorenzo slum district of Rome.

Did Montessori have experience with other "special" children, such as the mentally retarded?

Yes. For example, she directed the State Orthophrenic School for "deficient" children and taught there for two years. Some of her pupils were able to pass the state examinations in reading and writing for normal children. Some of these "deficient" children may have been those we would diagnose today as learning disabled or emotionally disturbed.

Can I do some Montessori in my home?

There are many Montessori-type activities and materials that you can provide for your child. There are a number of Montessori principles that you can apply at home, including ordering the environment, scaling down the environment, and respect for the child. (See the extensive suggestions for parents in Section Four of this book.) A home, however, can never duplicate the social interactions and the complete curriculum in a well-run Montessori classroom.

Can I order Montessori materials for my child to use at home?

This is not feasible. Besides the cost, there is the matter of the training required for the adult who is to demonstrate the materials. However, one can make some Montessori-type materials at a reasonable cost.

How about the "Montessori" kits and learning games one sees for sale?

Montessorians are divided on the issue of the usefulness of these commercially available items. Shop discriminatingly. Many bear no resemblance to any material used in a Montessori classroom. Check with your local Montessori school for guidance.

2. Maria Montessori: A Biographical Sketch

Maria Montessori was born in Chiaravalle, Italy, in 1870. Her parents moved to Rome, where she was graduated from the University of Rome at the age of twenty-six with a degree in medicine and surgery—the first woman to complete medical training in Italy. As an assistant doctor at the University Psychiatric Clinic, she became interested in the plight of the "deficient" children who in those days were placed with adults in insane asylums. She studied the educational methods of Edouard Seguin (1812–1880), himself a pupil of Jean Itard (1775–1838), both of whom were French physician-educators who worked with handicapped children. Today they are considered two of the foremost pioneers in special education.

Montessori saw mental deficiency as an educational rather than a medical problem. After lecturing to Roman teachers on special education, she became director of the State Orthophrenic School for deficient children; she taught there for two years while supervising the other teachers. She also traveled abroad to study the special-education techniques in use in other countries.

Some of Montessori's pupils from the Orthophrenic School who had been classified as retarded were able to pass the state examinations in reading and writing for normal children. While observers were admiring these miraculous results, Montessori searched for the

33

reasons that her deficient pupils could equal normal children in the tests. She decided that her pupils had been able to compete successfully only because they had been taught differently. Her children had been helped in their psychic development, while the normal pupils in the regular schools had, in effect, been hampered—suffocated, as she put it. Montessori believed that if the educational methods that had helped her children were applied to normal children, the results would be even more startling. Several years later she was to have the opportunity to test this idea.

In the meantime, she took additional courses at the University of Rome and conducted research with children in the elementary schools. This work led to a teaching position at the university from 1904 to 1908. She also held the chair of hygiene at the Magistero Femminile in Rome (one of the two Italian women's colleges of the time).

Montessori wanted to test her methods with a class of normal children. The chance came in 1906, when the director of the Roman Association for Good Building asked her to establish a school for the young children of working parents in one of the association's tenament buildings. These buildings in the San Lorenzo slum district had been hastily and shoddily constructed during a short-lived boom and were in poor repair. The association, in attempting to rehabilitate them, found that the children of working parents were vandalizing the property.

The plan was to gather these children in a large room where their activities would be under the supervision of a teacher throughout the day. The teacher was to live in an apartment in the building. If this initial class proved effective, the program was to be expanded.

The first Casa dei Bambini ("House of Children") was officially opened on January 6, 1907. Three months later a second opened nearby, and soon more were starting in other districts and cities for children of all socioeconomic levels. Montessori's book, *Metodo della Pedagogia Scientifica applicato all'educazione infantile nelle Casa dei Bambini*, which described the highly successful results of her approach, appeared in 1909. She discussed the development of her method and its features, such as freedom, activity, observation, and self-discipline. Word of this "new education" spread rapidly, and educators embarked for Italy to see the method in action and to take training.

In the United States, S. S. McClure, editor of *McClure's* magazine sensed the significance of Montessori's work and in May 1911 started to publish a series of articles on it. The English-language edition of her book, under the title *The Montessori Method*, appeared in 1912. It was translated by Anne E. George, Montessori's first American teacher-trainee, who opened the first American Montessori school in Tarrytown, New York. In his introduction to the book, which became a best-seller, Professor Henry Holmes of Harvard University described Montessori's work as "remarkable, novel, and important." A wave of popular and professional books and articles about the Montessori method appeared in the United States and abroad.

In November 1913 she arrived in New York to begin a lecture tour, during which she met such distinguished persons as Alexander Graham Bell, Thomas Edison, Helen Keller, and John Dewey. A Montessori Association of America was soon formed, with Mrs. Bell as president and U.S. Commissioner of Education P. P. Claxton as vice-president. President Woodrow Wilson's daughter became a trustee.

Montessori returned to America in 1915 to give a summer course in San Francisco at the Panama-Pacific Exposition, a huge affair to celebrate the completion of the Panama Canal. Helen Parkhurst (who later developed the Dalton plan of education) directed a model Montessori class in a glass-walled enclosure in the vast Hall of Education. The children in this class received two gold medals, the only gold medals awarded at the exposition. The National Education Association's annual meeting in 1915 was cast in the form of an international congress on education held at Oakland, where Montessori delivered four addresses to the congress concerning her system of education.

Montessori never returned to the United States, but traveled to many other parts of the world. While she was interned in India during World War II, she established an Indian Montessori movement. She served as president of the Association Montessori Internationale (AMI), which was founded in 1929, until her death in the Netherlands on May 6, 1952, at the age of eighty-one.

Today there are Montessori schools, societies, and teacher-training programs in many countries throughout the world.

3. What Is Montessori?

The answer to this question is given here both in the context of some of the Montessori literature and of an imaginary visit to a Montessori school.

The primary goal of the Montessori approach is to serve as an "aid to life." It aims to help people master their environment rather than have the environment master them. It offers this help through strengthening people's capacities and adaptabilities, imparting knowledge, developing skills, and giving freedom to practice them.

This aid to life is not restricted to preprimary education. It extends into the primary and secondary stages and further, and into the home, helping the parent understand the child.

Robert Peary, the explorer, called Montessori's work "the discovery of the human soul." It was this discovery of the soul that made her work significant, not her curriculum. What, then, was the discovery? Two observations are of the greatest significance:

1. Given the correct educational environment, the child learns much more easily and earlier than was formerly thought possible. Information is gained through the child's activity and movement.
2. Given the correct structure and freedom within that environ-

ment, the child develops personality characteristics not usually associated with childhood. This is the process Montessori termed *normalization*.

The concept of normalization was an extremely significant discovery. A "normalized" child will love learning, be kind to others, develop concentration and work habits, and become independent. These traits, when developed early, are likely to stay with a child into adulthood.

Deviations from the normal may occur if a child is inhibited in his movements in spite of his will to act, or if the will of adults is unneccesarily substituted for that of the child. These deviations may manifest themselves in aggression, fantasy, or withdrawal. They may take the form of attachment to an adult, possessiveness, desire for power, inferiority complex, temper tantrums, or lying. For many children, the cure for these difficulties is attachment to working with something that brings success. Through success with a task of his own choosing, the child starts to feel better about himself and to demonstrate the characteristics of normalization.

Montessori regarded this discovery of the normal characteristics of childhood as the most important result of her work. Previously, unacceptable behavior was regarded as normal for children—as part of their inherent nature. But Montessori showed that children possess positive characteristics that are forced below the surface by their deviant development. Once the child was treated with respect and care, his positive characteristics of consideration and love of learning emerged.

When observing a child, we must appreciate the life force that is at work. There is a plan within each child for development. We must provide activity, freedom to follow his own rhythm, the opportunity to choose his work and to remain at the task as long as he chooses, and the opportunity to practice. The work of the child is to construct a person adapted to his environment, time, place, and culture.

The needs of the child should determine the curriculum. Each child must be respected, observed, and allowed to grow. The program for the child must be individualized, tailored to meet the child's needs at all times.

Montessori divided human development into four stages. The needs of people are different during each of these stages, and the environment should be prepared accordingly. The four stages of development are separated into the ages from birth to six, six to twelve, twelve to eighteen, and eighteen to twenty-four. The first three years of each period are a stage of growth; the second three years are a refinement of that growth. The periods from birth to six and twelve to eighteen are the periods of greatest change, and they parallel each other. The period from six to twelve is one of regularity, of growth and developing reason, but not of transformation. During this period, the child can acquire a great deal of knowledge. During the twelve-to-fifteen period, the child should not be pushed, since being in puberty makes him as delicate as if he were in infancy. From fifteen to eighteen, the child should be prepared for taking his place in life by tutoring and vocational exploration. The eighteen-to-twenty-four period is the young-adult stage; by this time, the person should be as economically independent as possible, even if attending a college or university.

The birth-to-six period is the basis for the future, as it is during this time that the child is forming himself. Montessori believed that during this time, the child is a psychic embryo in the process of constructing a person from his environment according to his own needs of development. In the birth-to-six period, the greatest development of powers is from birth to the age of three; these powers are refined and extended from three to six.

The child's development from three to six will reflect the degree to which, from birth to the age of three, there has been freedom of choice, prepared environment, and removal of obstacles.

The birth-to-six period is also the period of what Montessori called the absorbent mind. From birth to three, the child has an unconscious absorbent mind; from three to six, his absorbent mind becomes conscious. The unconscious absorbent mind takes in the environment, making it a part of itself. The child does not will it—it just happens. The child's conscious absorbent mind is capable of using will in relation to his environment. He has a memory. He knows he knows.

The child also has sensitive periods which take place within the four stages of development and vary in length. During these times, a sensitivity toward a particular activity or acquisition of skill is revealed. The characteristics of a sensitive period remain for a while and then disappear. From observing children all over the world,

Montessori discovered that children have the same sensitive periods. The adult's task is to recognize the sensitivity and prepare the environment so that the child can achieve an optimum stage of development while the sensitive period is at its height. For instance, during the years from approximately one and a half to three and a half, the child passes through a sensitive period for order. If the adult orders the environment and shows the child how to maintain order, the child will be more likely to keep his room in order when he is fifteen than a child whose needs for order were neglected when he was two. After the sensitive period has passed, learning of that particular skill is a chore and not a normal part of development. If a sensitive period is not recognized, the opportunity is lost and the adult will not be as perfect in his development.

The Montessori curriculum is based on the sensitive periods of the absorbent mind. Each piece of apparatus has a purpose in strengthening the developing intellect through movement, especially with the hand, and helps to unite mind and body, creating an integrated person. The material is divided into four main areas: practical life, sensorial, language, and mathematics. Also included are geography, science, art, music, and movement activities.

The aim of the practical life material is to bring about an integrated personality (mind, body, spirit) through activities involving real work dealing with the child's culture. While he is polishing his shoes, for example, the child's mind is directing his body in logical, sequential actions. It is the development of this capacity to plan and follow through on a task that is the real product, not the clean shoes.

The aim of the sensorial material is to give the child the keys to exploration so that he can clarify and organize the impressions his mind already holds as well as sharpen the power of his senses. Working with the pink tower of ten size-graded cubes, the child clarifies his concept of *big* and *little* through his own activity and is also refining his ability to discriminate size with his vision and touch.

Utilizing scientific observation, Montessori established the beginnings of her science of humans and evolved a formula that aids human development. Some results will be obtained if the formula is not followed carefully, but they will not be the best. Those Montessori principles that have been found to be universally applicable are the *absorbent mind* and its functioning, the *sensitive periods of development*, the *importance of repetition*, the *need for the prepared environment, liberty leading to inner discipline,* and the *characteristics of normalization* including concentration, joy in work, and social development.

The Montessori method is not just a means to teach children intellectual accomplishments. The purpose of Montessori is to aid in the formation of people—the development of the child to adulthood. Montessori believed that education must help life.

Montessori's theories are used in education, but the discovery of true potential is actually a discovery in psychology with an application in sociology. The fundamental problem, as Montessori saw it, is to establish a better relationship between two estranged sections of society—adults and children. Adults and children have been waging war for generations. The child's mind, rhythm, and needs are different from those of adults. Since the child has been oppressed, his true nature has not been able to reveal itself. The fundamental difference between the child and the adult is that the child is in a continuous state of growth and metamorphosis, while the adult has achieved his growth. Montessori hoped that her work would help the child be understood.

As Montessori wrote in *The Absorbent Mind,* "We serve the future by protecting the present. The more fully the needs of one period are met, the greater will be the success of the next."

4. Montessori as Practiced
in a Normal Primary Montessori Class

Imagine you are in a large, well-lit room observing your first Montessori class. The furniture consists of small tables and chairs, low shelves, little rugs on the floor. There are plants, vases with flowers, books, pictures on the walls, materials on the shelves. Children, little ones—aged two and a half to six—are moving quietly about, choosing work from the shelves and taking it to a table or a mat on the floor.

The children seem to enjoy each other's company. Some laugh together as they work. A few are concentrating intensely on a project and do not seem to notice their peers. The children move about the room freely but carefully, and with purpose.

The adult, the teacher, is not noticeable at first. After observing a bit, you notice her sitting on the floor with a group of two or three of the youngest children, giving them a sandpaper-letter lesson. "This is *m*. Say *m*. Trace it. Like this." She guides the first two fingers of the pudgy hand over the letters. "What is this?" she asks the child. *M*, comes the self-assured answer. The rest of the children continue their work, seemingly without guidance, but clearly with purpose.

What are the children working on? You begin to notice the equipment. Two boys about four years old are working on a mat with a puzzle-map of Europe. "Can you find Germany?" one asks the oth-

43

er. A girl of about five is sitting by herself at a small table reading the list of words beginning with *sh*: "Ship, shin . . ." A boy of about two and half is finishing a table-washing exercise. He dries the bucket and basin and replaces the soap dishes and brush. It is all in order and ready for the next person. At age two and a half, he is in a sensitive period for order. Now he rolls up the mat, throws it up on his shoulder, and walks off to put it away. He is satisfied.

The teacher leaves the little ones with the sandpaper letters and moves to a group of four-and-a-half-year-olds, experienced enough to work with the bank game alone. They are being introduced to the decimal system and mathematical operations with Montessori beads. "Let's see what number you have made," she says. "Joan, you had 2323 and Rick had 2323 and Sam also had 2323. What was your answer when you added that all up?" Rick answers, "Six-nine-six-nine." "That's correct. And do you know what we call adding up the same number over and over?" "No," say the group. "We call that multiplication. And here is the sign that means to multiply." She shows them a laminated × sign from a plastic box on the shelf. "You discovered something new today. You discovered multiplication." "Let's do it again," says Joan. And they do.

The first visit to a regular Montessori class is always a pleasant shock. How can these little children be so self-directed? How can they learn so much more than is usually expected from such young people? Why aren't they fighting?

The answers to these questions are answers to What is Montessori?

First of all, the environment has been prepared carefully for the child by the teacher in accordance with Montessori's discoveries. Children, she observed, have certain tendencies toward movement, order, and exploration of the environment. They have a need to classify and clarify through their senses the random impressions they receive from their environment. Given the proper manipulation work, a structure for behavior, and the freedom to work uninterrupted for as long as they like, they become self-directed and develop an attention span and concentration. The teacher prepares the environment and curriculum to achieve these goals.

The Montessori curriculum includes work in practical life (caring for self and environment), sensorial development (clarifying and classifying impressions of color, shape, size, and so on), language (sandpaper-letter work leads to reading and writing), and mathematics (from quantity symbols to operations). Also included are geography, science, history, art, music, storytelling, milk and cookies, and outside play.

Second, as the small child works with his whole body or as his hands work with concrete objects, he starts to learn language and to think abstractly. "Oh, this is long and this is short." "Look, *m-a-t* says mat!" "Feel the land on the globe" (it is sandpaper), and "feel the water" (it is smooth blue paint). "We live on land. Where do I live?" Because the materials are in the environment and because the teacher links the child with the environment through presentations, the child learns easily and naturally. Older children teach younger ones. There is much quiet talk and movement.

Third, there is neither fighting nor possessiveness because of the ground rules of the class and the normalization of the children. Montessori coined the word *normalization* because she felt all children normally are kind to each other and eager to learn.

A normalized child will be joyful, confident, and self-directed. Love of learning and independence are the true products of the Montessori experience for a child; acquiring academic skills early is secondary. As the child masters the small environment of the classroom, he builds the skills needed to master the larger environment of the society in which he will be an adult.

5. The Role of the Directress

The primary role of the Montessori directress is not so much to teach as to direct the natural energy of the children. For this reason he or she is called a director or directress. The teacher unites with the "new children" to form a "new education" in which both children and teacher are in a continuous process of development, learning from each other.

Her responsibility is to care for the classroom—the environment—to know the needs of the child and present the materials with such exactness that he can further his development through repetitive work with them.

Montessori likened the relationship of teacher and child to that of valet and master, noting, "The master whom the teacher serves is the child's spirit; when it shows its needs she must hasten to respond to them."

The teacher's first task is to prepare the environment. In order to do this she must have a full understanding of the children: their sensitive periods, age characteristics, and planes of development. It is necessary to prepare an environment in which the child can develop with a minimum of error. She must strive for perfection in dealing with the materials for the children, as nothing is too good for the children. All objects in the environment must be scaled down to the

47

children's size. There must be a plan behind the furnishing of the environment, a sequence, and an awareness of beauty, form, and order. Each object must have its own place on the shelf. The teacher herself must be tidy and pleasing.

The teacher is responsible for maintaining order in the environment. Each child should be trained to return his work to the shelf when he is finished with it. It is essential to give the child sufficient time to pack up. The teacher is the link between the children and the environment. She must put them into contact with each other.

Next comes the second task or stage: group exercises leading the child to control and precision of movement. When movement is becoming controlled, the teacher may begin on individual presentations and enter into the third stage, in which the children show interest in the work and develop concentration.

Before giving a presentation of any teaching material, the teacher obtains the child's consent. When the directress is presenting a piece of apparatus to a child, she must do it slowly and precisely, so that the child can learn what that material has to offer. "An adult," wrote Montessori, "if he is to afford the proper guidance, must always be calm and act slowly so that the child who is watching him can clearly see his actions in all their particulars." The teacher must demonstrate exercises quietly. The child should focus on the exercise, not on the teacher. After the child shows he is interested in the material, she may leave the child alone with it.

It is the teacher's duty to protect and foster the whole development of the child. She should not dominate or abandon him. She must know how much she can control without dominating and how much she can withdraw without abandoning. She should be invisible as a personality, but must be there as a person.

The teacher has to acquire the power of silence as well as facility in speech. And, instead of teaching, she has to observe. In fact, the fundamental quality of the directress is the capacity for observation.

The teacher needs love, humility, gentleness, compassion, a sense of humor, and awareness of her own limitations.

There must be love between each child and the teacher, but she must never seek children's affection or gratitude. It is easy to make children slaves to adult affection. The children must be attached to the work, not to the adult's approval. She should not hug them or take them on her knee unless there is a need for it.

In the matter of discipline, the teacher does not expect obedience simply because she has given an order. She must think about a command carefully before giving it. She gives her command from love, not from authority, and disciplines according to the needs of each child.

If a rule is made, it should be one that is essential to the order of the class, and then it must be insisted upon. It is important not to correct children's behavior unless it is necessary, but the teacher should correct the children every time they commit impolite and disorderly actions, that is, actions that do not spring from a good impulse or that may do harm. She should not only intervene when there is disorder, immediately and even forcefully, but she should also act beforehand to prevent its coming. Usually she should not interfere in disputes, as they often settle themselves. If intervention is necessary, she should hear both sides.

The teacher should never enter into an argument with a child or show anger. She must remain calm and dispassionate. She must never punish in anger. The child will accept punishment that is fair and just. The teacher does not surrender authority; she leads rather than drives.

The principle of nonintervention is vital, in that the teacher must know when to interfere and when not to. Part of her task is to remove obstacles from the path of the child's development. She herself can be the child's greatest obstacle if she intervenes at the wrong time. Before deciding on a course of action, she must wait to observe what the child is really doing, as a child's actions are often misunderstood by adults.

She must not interfere with an action when the impulse that prompted it is a good one. Her intervention will destroy the impulse or cause the child to withdraw into himself. If the child is making a mistake, she should use indirect correction later on. For example, if a child is painting a sky with poster paints and inadvertently mixes the blue for the sky with the yellow for the sun and green sky results, the teacher should observe, but not correct. To call attention to the child's mistake immediately would cause the child to be defensive, to lose self-esteem and perhaps result in removing the child's desire to try painting again. Later the teacher should give a general lesson, without calling attention to that particular child, on how to paint with two colors and keep them distinct.

Children need to be treated with respect and sensitivity. Harsh correction usually does more harm than good. It is better to teach and reteach than to correct.

In summary, the teacher serves the child. She prepares the environment, creating an orderly, attractive, and interesting classroom. She establishes the structure or ground rules for behavior and sees that they are followed. She gives individual and group lessons on the use of materials. She frees the child, within the structure of the classroom, to move, to talk, to make choices, and to become interested in working with the materials.

The teacher strives to aid in the development of an independent, active, capable child. As he increases in power, she seeks a more passive role for herself, diminishing her role as the child expands his.

SECTION TWO

Learning Disabilities

6. Learning Disabilities and Montessori: Questions and Answers

What are learning disabilities?

First, it should be pointed out that *learning disabilities* is often used interchangeably with *specific learning disabilities*.

The most official definition of specific learning disabilities is that incorporated in the Education of the Handicapped Act (Public Law 91-230):

"The term *children with specific learning disabilities* means those children who have a disorder in one or more of the basic psychological processes involved in understanding or in using language, spoken or written, which disorder may manifest itself in imperfect ability to listen, think, speak, read, write, spell, or do mathematical calculations. Such disorders include such conditions as perceptual handicaps, brain injury, minimal brain dysfunction, dyslexia, and developmental aphasia. Such term does not include children who have learning problems which are primarily the result of visual, hearing, or motor handicaps, of mental retardation, of emotional disturbance, or of environmental disadvantage."

Put more simply, a child with a learning disability is one who is of average or above-average intelligence, who is not learning as he should, and whose learning problems are not caused by physical, emotional, or environmental factors.

So children with learning disabilities are not mentally retarded?

Correct. However, some children who are mentally retarded have learning problems in addition to their limited intellectual abilities and respond to some of the same methods used to teach learning-disabled children.

It is also recognized that severe learning problems often prevent children from scoring well on intelligence tests. Sometimes, then, a learning-disabled child will score in the borderline mentally retarded range even though his potential is higher. Most psychologists are alert to this and are careful not to diagnose a child as mentally retarded in spite of his score on an IQ test if it is suspected that learning problems are masking his potential.

Are learning-disabled children emotionally disturbed?

Not surprisingly, because of the frustrations associated with their difficulties in learning, many children with learning disabilities develop emotional disturbances in varying degrees.

However, as the federal definition above indicates, if a child's learning problems are primarily the result of emotional disturbance, he does not fit the definition.

What are the symptoms of learning disability?

Observable symptoms include:

1. academic failure
2. short attention span
3. frustration
4. difficulty in making and/or keeping friends
5. hyperactivity
6. behavior problem or withdrawal
7. poor muscular control

Many children go through a period of difficulty in one or more of these areas, so having problems in some of these areas does not necessarily mean a child is learning-disabled. In order for a diagnosis to be made, a child should be observed and tested by a psychologist, an educational diagnostician, or, preferably, a diagnostic team. The steps of discovery through diagnosis are covered in more detail in Section Four.

What causes learning disabilities?

Most experts speak of children with learning disabilities as having a neurological immaturity or handicap. This causes uneven development in perceptual, integration, and communication skills. Neurological immaturity may or may not show up in a medical examination. In any case, although the diagnosis may be medical, the prescription is usually educational. The child must be taught according to his strengths and weaknesses in order to achieve the potential he has.

Simply stated, a child with a learning disability is having difficulty processing information. Trouble is occurring in the input, integration, or output phases. Input comes through the visual (what he sees), auditory (what he hears), or tactile (what he feels) channels. A child may have perfect acuity in vision or hearing and still not see or hear the true message correctly. He has a perceptual problem. Integration of information includes thinking, recalling facts, and formulating a response. Output takes the form of communication, as in spoken and written language, or may be actions, such as throwing a ball or closing a door.

Often we hear the terms *dyslexia, minimal brain dysfunction,* and *specific learning disabilities.* All describe the problems of a child who is not learning up to his potential and must have special teaching to meet his special needs.

How many children with learning disabilities are there in this country?

According to the U.S. Office of Education, an estimated 1 to 3 percent of the United States population between the ages of three and twenty-one have such disorders, which means more than two million persons in this age range are affected. It should be noted that some authorities believe that 20 to 30 percent of the persons in this age range are affected significantly enough to be identified as having a learning disability.

What is the federal government doing about learning disabilities?

Under Public Law 91-230, Part G, the Bureau of Education for the Handicapped (BEH) of the U.S. Office of Education operates a learning-disabilities program. As part of this program, federal funds are used to create a number of model demonstration centers for the improvement of educational services for learning-disabled children.

What do these centers accomplish?

The federally funded Child Service Demonstration Centers (CSDC), using a variety of approaches to identify, diagnose, and prescribe services for learning-disabled children, attempt to stimulate the states and localities to increase the quality and quantitity of their services to these children. The centers demonstrate the feasibility of various programs; the aim is for these model programs to be copied as and where they are needed.

What do the centers emphasize?

They focus upon (1) model program planning, operation, and evaluation; (2) early identification of learning-disabled children and the provision of diagnostic-prescriptive services; (3) coordination with community agencies and schools; (4) advisory council activities; (5) parent participation; (6) planned stimulation of new programs; (7) dissemination of new methods and techniques for overcoming learning disabilities.

How can I learn more about the work of these demonstration centers?

Write to:

Coordinator, Learning Disabilities Program
Bureau of Education for the Handicapped
Office of Education
Department of Health, Education and Welfare
Washington, D.C. 20202

Ask for a mailing list of all centers. The centers will send descriptive material at your request.

Where can I get more information on learning disabilities that would be helpful to parents?

One source of brochures and other useful, inexpensive materials is:

Association for Children with Learning Disabilities
5225 Grace Street
Pittsburgh, Pennsylvania 15236

Write for their price list.

What else is the federal government doing for children with learning disabilities?

Under Public Law 94-142, all children between the ages of three and twenty-one with handicapping conditions, including learning disabilities, are entitled to a free and appropriate education. This law means that children who are not learning as they should will be evaluated, planned for, and educated. The parent and, when appropriate, the child are included in the planning along with the teacher and resource personnel such as psychologists and speech therapists.

In the past, some learning-disabled children had been neglected, since there were no special classes available in the public schools or places in existing special classes, and many parents could not afford private-school tuition. This meant that many children were not receiving the education they needed. They were left in regular classes where they often became behavior problems or withdrew. Worse yet, many were misdiagnosed as retarded and were placed in classes that harmed rather than helped them.

Most educators regard Public Law 94-142 as a milestone for all handicapped children. It provides for the parent to be included in the planning and evaluation of his child's education and gives him the right to appeal if he believes the education offered is not appropriate. It gives the parent more responsibility and control over the education of his child and guarantees an education for every child.

Is there any one method that is always successful or best in teaching learning-disabled children?

Not to the authors' knowledge. Montessori, adapted to the needs of these children, has proved useful. It is one answer—but not the only answer. Why Montessori is applicable and how it has been modified in teaching learning-disabled children is explained in this book.

Are there any aspects or features of Montessori that do not readily lend themselves to work with the learning-disabled child?

The movement and conversation of a regular Montessori class of twenty-five to thirty children and a complete environment of materials is too distracting for most learning-disabled children. A learning-disabled child needs an environment with reduced stimuli.

A modified Montessori environment with ten to twelve children, places to go to be alone, and selected apparatus has proved to be a good approach.

What is the Montessori method for teaching reading? How is it used for the learning-disabled child?

Briefly, the Montessori method for teaching reading is a phonics approach.

The child first learns the sounds of the alphabet with the sandpaper letters (single letters made of sandpaper mounted on board). He traces the letter, says the sound, and sees the letter. After the child knows several sounds, the teacher dictates phonetic words (*mom, run, jump*) which the child forms on a mat on the floor using cutout letters from a box (movable alphabet). Soon he starts to write the words and read them. Work with the sandpaper letters and movable alphabet continues for several months. The child is then introduced to blending sounds, (for example, *j-e-t*) and sight words (words which follow no set rule, for example, *the*). Soon he is able to read simple books and progresses happily from these to more advanced books.

For the learning-disabled child, the method is used for diagnosis (does he know the sounds of the alphabet?) and then takes the child forward from the stage at which he is already learning. A child who can write will take dictation of phonetic words with paper and pencil instead of the movable alphabet. A child who cannot write on paper at a desk will take dictation on the blackboard or at a table high enough for him to stand at.

As a learning-disabled child progresses in reading and gains confidence, he is given an opportunity to make a second try with traditional reading materials such as readers and workbooks. The teacher keeps the child's learning needs in mind. For example, if he has visual perception problems (difficulty seeing correctly), the teacher will place a marker under the line of print he is reading; this will guide his eyes and give him a better chance of success.

Montessori, then, is a good tool for diagnosing reading problems and for giving basic skill and confidence. When a child is going to return to a regular class, he is introduced to the materials used in that class.

Is Montessori suitable for all learning-disabled children?

The approach works with children who have difficulty seeing and hearing correctly (visual and auditory perception problems) and with those who have difficulty using their bodies in a coordinated manner, using their hands easily, or using their hands and eyes together. Since Montessori is multisensory, it allows the child to work with his strongest learning channel.

Hyperactive children usually do well in an adapted Montessori classroom with a structure for behavior and fewer children and things. Within the rules, they are free to move and explore and change position as they work. Not all their energy is going into sitting still. They are free to learn.

Montessori also works with children with mild to moderate emotional and social problems. It is less successful with those children whose primary need is intensive psychiatric therapy; sometimes the classroom instruction must be supplemented with additional speech, motor, psychological, or psychiatric therapy.

How can one identify children with learning disabilities early, without the harmful effects of labeling them?

It is not necessary to label a young child to observe his learning strengths and weaknesses and to make plans to teach him accordingly. For instance, a teacher may notice that a child learns best if he can touch the things about which he is learning rather than by just listening to an explanation. In that case, she will give him an opportunity to touch objects and to use his hands in his learning.

If a child of six or seven, for example, is not learning to read and does not respond in spite of the teacher's best efforts, or if he has a short attention span, does not follow directions, and has difficulty getting along with his classmates, the teacher may make a referral to a diagnostician for testing for learning problems.

Although labeling a child is harmful if the label is used to call him hopeless or unmanageable, greater harm will come to the child if his learning problems are ignored, left undiagnosed and untreated. Then he may become angry and frustrated, and by the time he is an unachieving teenager, he may become delinquent or severely emotionally disturbed due to repeated failure.

It is important not to use labeling as an excuse for not teaching a child. Rather, we must identify his learning needs so that we can teach him better.

To what extent should learning-disabled children be taught with normal children? There is much talk these days of keeping the special child in normal classes.

Learning-disabled children should be taught with normal children whenever possible. However, the learning-disabled child's time is at a premium, and he should be in an environment that optimizes his chance of learning. If this environment includes normal children, so much the better. If the child needs a small, structured class with a minimum of distractions, that is where he should be placed. After learning to learn, and after he has had some academic success, he should be returned to a normal classroom.

What rewards and satisfactions can Montessori teachers reasonably expect in working with learning-disabled children?

A learning-disabled child has average or above-average intelligence and a desire to learn. When he is taught so that he can be successful, he becomes increasingly confident and a joy to teach. When he finally learns a skill, his pleasure is a precious gift to his teacher.

When he is taught so that he can learn, the learning-disabled child likes school for the first time, his behavior improves, and his self-esteem blossoms. Seeing the child achieve is a reward for every teacher.

What problems and special demands does such work involve?

Working with learning-disabled youngsters is a very demanding task. It requires all the intellectual, physical, and emotional stamina a teacher has. The teacher must be constantly alert to the child's needs and must be able to modify her approach to meet them.

Teachers report that their minds are always working on the problems their students present. Often the children are the last thing they think about before sleeping and their first concern in the morning.

How can a Montessori teacher best prepare for teaching such children?

Before a Montessori teacher begins working with children who have learning problems, she must have experience in a regular Montessori classroom, so that she knows her curriculum thoroughly and knows how normal children react to it. She will also need training in special education and should be certified to teach such classes in the state in which she works.

In teaching learning-disabled youngsters, she will need to modify and simplify some of the lessons to allow them to succeed. She will need to integrate some public school curriculum into the Montessori curriculum in order to prepare children for return to public or private school.

Can a teacher realistically be expected to have all the qualities that Montessori desires?

No. No one is perfect. We can all try to observe the child, respect his individuality, and prepare the environment for him. We will not always succeed.

Teaching is a demanding profession; no human being can be humble and patient always. It is important that teachers are free to express their fears and negative feelings in confidence to a supervisor or fellow teacher. We all need support and understanding. Once these feelings are expressed, most teachers continue to do a good job with children.

What can the public school teacher do to apply Montessori to learning-disabled children in her class?

The public school teacher can observe each child carefully so as to be able to meet his particular needs, individualize her approach, structure and simplify tasks, give opportunities for working with manipulable learning materials, and use well-timed praise.

What can the teacher, Montessori or otherwise, who is working with learning-disabled children, do to prevent discipline problems from arising?

Teach for success. Discipline problems decrease when the child is learning and feels happy with himself.

Once a child is interested in what he is doing, he becomes absorbed in the task, his attention span increases, and his concentration develops. To achieve this, the teacher must provide structure for behavior and freedom of choice within that structure.

When discipline problems occur, what are the most effective means of coping with them?

There are two basic approaches, which work with most children:

Attach the child to you. Keep the troubled or troublesome child close so he can feel the security of your presence. As his need for this closeness lessens, he will gradually detach himself from you.

Remove the child to a quiet area until he can discuss what is bothering him; help the child express and understand his feelings. Give him quiet reassurance that you understand he finds it difficult to control his behavior, but you believe he can do it.

Given the proper, special learning environment and teaching, do learning-disabled children always progress, acquire control over their bodies and emotions, and enjoy learning? Are there ever lapses into apathy and tantrums?

Even with the best teaching and school environment, the progress of learning-disabled children is not smooth. There are sometimes lapses into anger and withdrawal. Learning-disabled children have markedly uneven abilities, and this often causes frustration for them.

When a lapse occurs, the teacher must double her patience and her efforts. She must watch carefully to determine the reason behind the lapse and attempt to correct it. For instance, a child may get angry when asked to do math problems in his workbook. He may tear up the page or hide his book or simply look out the window. He may even throw the book or attempt to strike out at the teacher. If this occurs, it is probably because he is unable to do the work required even if he did the previous page successfully and without incident.

It is the teacher's responsibility to remind the child gently that such behavior is unacceptable and then ask about or observe the reason for the behavior. If the work is too difficult, she must reteach the task, breaking it down into easily understood steps. It is best to use materials which the child can touch and therefore understand more easily.

Children do not progress smoothly. There will be plateaus and lapses. And there also will be leaps forward.

What progress is made by children with learning disabilities? Do they ever catch up with children their own age? What are they like when they grow up?

If they are taught correctly, most such children eventually catch up with children of their own age. They can and do learn reading, mathematics, spelling, writing, and the other academic subjects. Behavior problems decrease once success is established. Learning-disabled youngsters usually become independent and useful adults.

Many youngsters who are not discovered as being learning-disabled develop behavior problems which cause a cycle of anger and failure. These youngsters often become delinquent adolescents and/ or adults with marginal skills for employment.

There are many adults who had undiscovered learning disabilities and who are functioning well in society. However, these adults were probably the children who were always in trouble in school, the ones who could never quite learn to read, and who spent many of their days in the principal's office. They would have been much happier in school and would have achieved more of their potential if they had been taught according to their strengths and weaknesses.

How can Montessori be made more available to learning-disabled children? Only a tiny fraction of such children now benefit from this approach.

Parents can ask that the approach be used with their learning-disabled children. Montessorians can engage in dialogue with public school teachers. Teachers of children with learning disabilities can observe in Montessori schools. In general, open communication between parents, teachers, and school administrators smooths the path to using successful approaches with learning-disabled children.

7. From Learning Disabilities to Learning Abilities with Montessori: Case Histories

Learning abilities can be broken down into categories. All people possess varying degrees of ability in each category. A child with a marked deficit over time in one or more areas is considered learning-disabled.

In order to teach a child with learning problems, the educator must know both the strengths and the weaknesses of the child and teach to the strong areas while building skills in the weak areas.

For instance, for a child with auditory strengths (able to learn best through listening) but visual weaknesses (not able to understand or remember what he sees), the most effective teaching will occur in verbal rather than written form. While presenting oral lessons—stories, discussions, lectures—so that the child can learn, the teacher also gives exercises to increase visual skills. The child is learning content through oral work and at the same time building the visual skill he needs to learn more easily.

If a child has mild difficulty in one area, it does not automatically mean that he is learning-disabled. However, if a child is not learning at a level reasonably close to his potential, testing and diagnosis may reveal weaknesses in one or more of the following areas:

gross motor development
fine motor abilities
sensory-motor integration
visual discrimination
auditory discrimination
tactile discrimination
specific learning disabilities
conceptual skills
social relationships
emotional adjustment
developmental delay

The following case histories illustrate how individual programs can be developed to remediate disabilities in each of these areas.

GROSS MOTOR DEVELOPMENT

(Development and coordinated use of the large muscles. Awareness of the body. Example: The child can roll, sit, walk, throw, jump, etc., and can name parts of body.)

Case History

William was a seven-and-a-half-year-old who had had difficulty with academic tasks since nursery school. He was not learning to read. He was hyperactive (unable to sit quietly for any length of time).

Psychological testing indicated that William was functioning in the superior range of intelligence in speech but scored badly in the performance or motor-related areas (skills that require coordinated movement of the body). He could not use his eyes and body together easily in a task like jumping on one spot or catching a ball. He could not tell how parts of a puzzle fit together and could not use his hands in small tasks like cutting or tracing. He appeared to learn easily through listening and discussing, but his difficulty with the use of his hands kept him from working at a level equal to his potential.

After William was placed in a special school, further testing revealed pronounced weakness in gross motor abilities. He was unable to name and point to the parts of his body. He could not tell right from left. He could not hop on one foot, walk a balance beam, or skip. When asked to sit on the floor with his legs crossed, he lost his balance and fell backward. His parents reported that he often dropped things, fell, and was clumsy.

Since William was not sure where his body was in space or in which direction he was moving, it was not surprising that he did not know on which side of the page to start reading and could not distinguish b from d. In order to correct his reversals and omissions in reading, the school had to start with his body.

William had good verbal ability. He was able to understand what was said to him, think about it, speak clearly, and express his thoughts. Since this was a definite learning strength, he was taught new facts and ideas through discussions and stories. While he continued to learn through his hearing, his teachers worked on strengthening his awareness of his own body and its position in space. To increase his coordination, he did exercises with balance beams, rocker boards, *Stegel*, trampoline, and directed ball play.

At age nine, William can hop, run, and climb. He knows right from left on his body. He can even hit a ball with a bat if it is pitched slowly. He can sit comfortably on the floor with his legs crossed and is less hyperactive. His reading ability also has improved. Although he still must sometimes remind himself where to start on a page, he now reads for pleasure and is near his grade level. He has returned to public school.

FINE MOTOR ABILITIES

(Development and coordinated use of the small muscles of the hand. Example: Child can eat neatly, draw, cut, trace, write.)

Case History

Sarah was referred to the Montessori Resource Room because she was unable to write in cursive at the age of fifteen. She had recently entered the special school after a frustrating time in public school. She had withdrawn from most social contact and had been truant.

Testing revealed near-average intelligence. Special tests for learning abilities and disabilities revealed that she had difficulty using her hands and eyes together and using her hands in a smooth, coordinated manner. Her movements were jerky and inconsistently controlled. She had difficulty listening to and following directions and telling the difference between sounds. Sarah had good use of her vision in getting accurate information from her environment. She could figure out things best by using visual clues. In spite of poor coordination, she also learned by touching. Her self-concept had suffered from learning problems and frustration due to failure. Counseling was recommended if Sarah did not start to feel better about herself.

In the Montessori Resource Room, the teaching of cursive began with large sandpaper letters individually mounted on small boards. Sarah was shown how to trace a letter and say its sound as she traced it, using her senses of sight, hearing, and touch at the same time. Once she could trace a letter easily, she wrote it large on the blackboard, first while looking and then with her eyes averted. This practice with the movements of her hand (kinesthetic movement) led to her writing letters fairly automatically. Then she went on to writing on paper with wide red lines with a felt-tip pen, and gradually worked toward using narrower lines and smaller cursive writing.

As her skill in writing improved, Sarah became less tense and her feelings of failure diminished. With increased confidence, she was more comfortable with other children and liked school for the first time.

SENSORY-MOTOR INTEGRATION

(Ability of the mind to direct movement of body and hands and carry out its intention in a smooth and coordinated manner. Example: The child can follow spoken commands, knows right from left, is aware of the concept of time, and can move through the classroom and other environments with ease and care.)

Case History

Alice was five when she entered a special Montessori preschool class of eight children. She had been asked to leave her nursery school because of behavior problems. She would not obey and could not play well with others. Although she tried very hard, she could not remember even the simplest nursery rhymes or songs.

Testing revealed normal intelligence. Her poor adjustment to the nursery school was caused by a number of learning disabilities which were revealed by testing. Alice did not receive the correct messages from spoken language (auditory reception), which explained her inability to remember rhymes and songs. She did not know top from bottom, front from back, or up from down (spatial relationships), which made it difficult for her to understand her environment and how she fit into it. She did not understand the concept of time (temporal confusion). She did not understand the difference between a week and a day and was unable to "wait a few minutes" because she could not distinguish a few minutes from a week or a few hours.

Because she did not know where her body was in space, she often hurried through tasks in class, bumping into people and things. To lessen her feeling of confusion, she stayed near the teacher and wanted to sit in her lap and be hugged. She was a frightened, confused little girl.

In class, she was given lessons by demonstration; the teacher showed her each step of the task carefully. Quiet praise and the teacher's calm presence helped her. She succeeded in doing the simple sequential tasks of the beginning practical life exercises: polishing, buttoning, and pouring. Once she was able to accomplish these tasks, she progressed to the table-washing exercise, which consists of over fifty steps and required remembering the steps (sequencing), and using the large muscles of her body and the small muscles of her hands. Most of all, it required her to think about what she wanted her body to do and to remember to move carefully so as not to spill a bucket of water or bump into a classmate. Her mind, then, was directing her body in a task and in her movement through the environment. She was able to slow her movements and succeed in doing her work.

The order in the environment helped Alice order herself. Her parents helped by simplifying her environment at home and giving each possession a special place. The routine of each day was established; since Alice could anticipate what was going to happen next, some of her anxiety and, therefore, her behavior problems, decreased.

With Alice better able to anticipate the sequence of activities in a task or in a day, her ability to remember commands and rhymes increased. She became calmer and ready to learn.

Alice is now in a special Montessori class and attends it for the full day. At six and a half, she is starting to blend letters into words and to read, but she is still in need of a calm, protective structure for a while longer.

VISUAL DISCRIMINATION

(The ability to correctly perceive objects, forms, and symbols such as letters in the environment. This includes the ability to understand and interpret what is seen, to differentiate forms, to discriminate between background and foreground, and to remember what is seen. Example: Child can read from a page with his eyes moving from left to right and can understand the words he has read. He is able to screen out the illustrations, the page number, and the words he is not reading at the moment. He does not confuse b and d, h and n, saw and was.)

Case History

Dick, age six, was behind in kindergarten. He was unable to keep up with the lessons and was unhappy. His teacher recommended testing. The pediatrician diagnosed that he had possible minor brain damage (minimal brain dysfunction) and a one-year lag in using his eyes and body together (visual-motor development) and in using the small muscles of his hand (fine motor development).

The psychological evaluation revealed an inattentive and hyperactive boy whose intellectual, perceptual, and emotional development were uneven. The result was a low frustration level and a poor self-concept. An educational evaluation indicated that Dick had learning disabilities in using his eyes to gain information (visual discrimination) and in using his hands and body in a coordinated manner. It was recommended that he should be placed in a small special class and reevaluated in six months' time.

Dick was placed in a Montessori class of less than ten students. He instantly liked the sensorial equipment for size and form discrimination and would often choose equipment such as the geometry cabinet and repeat the task voluntarily. When he worked with these materials, he would be satisfied and appear calmer. He also liked materials extending discrimination skills, such as parquetry blocks. When the sandpaper letters were introduced, Dick traced them and soon was able to remember the letters and began to write them. He liked to match pictures of prehistoric animals, became curious about them and asked for stories about their lives. The puzzle-maps became a favorite; he was excellent at doing the map of Europe.

Reevaluation revealed that he was able to tell the difference between sizes, forms, letters, and words. He was able to discriminate visually; working at the Montessori equipment with his hands had given his brain the correct clues and feedback about size and shape. Now he could tell what things looked like with his eyes alone. In addition, he had become more dextrous. As a result of his work with puzzles, polishing, and geometric forms, with practice he was able to cut, trace, draw, and write. His learning abilities in the visual and fine motor areas had improved, and so he was acquiring academic skills more easily.

His self-concept had improved. Dick was learning to read with confidence. He is now in the second grade of public school, with a good teacher who is careful to insure his continued success. His parents will continue to make certain Dick has the teaching he needs.

AUDITORY DISCRIMINATION

(Ability to correctly perceive sounds and spoken words in the environment. This includes the ability to understand and interpret what is heard, to differentiate between sounds, to screen out the essential from the inessential in the environment, and to remember what is heard. Example: Child can listen to speech, hear correctly what is being said, and understand it. He can listen to a direction, understand what is being told, and remember it. He can listen to and tell the difference between a jet engine and thunder and between the short vowels *a* and *i*, e.g., *hat, hit*.)

Case History

Randy, age nine, had brain damage and so had always needed special schooling. His parents had removed him from his last school because they believed it was disorganized, noisy, and not meeting his needs. Even in the special school, Randy was unhappy and was not learning. He had not learned to read or write.

Testing by a speech pathologist revealed that Randy had difficulties in speech, fine motor control, and auditory and visual perception. Psychological testing showed that Randy had average intelligence but that his brain damage was causing hyperactivity. He was infantile and impulsive. An active fantasy life was emerging. Testing showed a need for a small, structured, special school class to help him overcome the problems brought about by the brain damage.

Randy was placed in a small, structured Montessori classroom of less than ten students. Because of his speech and hearing problems, he had speech therapy twice a week with the staff speech pathologist. Randy was especially sensitive to auditory distractions in his environment. He heard everything—airplanes, voices in another room, water running, the teacher's instructions. Everything he heard had the same importance to him. He could not screen out inessential sounds so as to be able to listen to the teacher and remember what she said.

He often appeared to misbehave, since he could not remember and follow a direction. Often in the process of following instructions he would forget or become distracted and fail to do what was required of him.

In class, Randy worked with the materials for discrimination of size and form, learning to see correctly and understand what he saw. To improve his coordination he did exercises in the form of games, such as jumping on the trampoline, running through obstacle courses, and walking on a line on the floor. He was given play therapy by the staff psychologist so that he could express his frustrations in therapy rather than in the classroom. Family counseling was recommended so that his parents could more clearly understand the cause of the problems Randy was presenting at home.

The problem of hearing and understanding (auditory discrimination) and remembering what he heard (auditory memory) were treated by:

1. Providing him with a quiet, nonstimulating place to work in the classroom
2. Giving him a one-step instruction and gradually building to two steps, three steps, and so on

3. Providing exercises in listening to and identifying familiar sounds in the environment

4. Providing games in which he localized sound

5. Getting him to sing songs and say rhymes to lengthen auditory memory

6. Having him listen to stories

With the limits and the calm, accepting structure of the classroom, Randy's behavior improved, and he started to learn to read. His fantasy life faded as he became more successful in reality. After two years, he was offered a place in a learning-disability class in a public school. Because of the severity of his learning problems, Randy has continued to need the individual attention and structure of a special class.

TACTILE DISCRIMINATION

(Ability to correctly perceive articles touched. Example: Child can use his sense of touch to tell the difference between size, shape, and texture. When he is blindfolded or with his eyes averted, he can discriminate between velvet and denim and between coarse and fine sandpaper.)

Case History

Christina was seven when she entered the special Montessori class. She did not know any of the sounds of the alphabet and did not know how to count. She was clumsy and did not like to be touched.

Observation during the first part of her enrollment revealed that she could not pick up a knobbed cylinder by the knob, only by the body of the cylinder. She was unable to hold a pencil or a crayon. She could not distinguish rough texture from smooth. When using her hands, she did not use the tips of her fingers.

Testing revealed that she was in a dull-normal range of intelligence and had difficulty understanding what she saw and heard. To improve her tactile discrimination, she was offered enjoyable lessons in stereognostic discrimination, that is, feeling objects while blindfolded and identifying them by touch only. She moved from identifying common objects to identifying solid geometric shapes, different-sized buttons, different grains. When she started to use the tips of her fingers, exercises in tactile discrimination were added. She learned the difference between rough and smooth texture, worked with wooden cards covered with graded textures of sandpaper, and then matched pairs of swatches of fabric while blindfolded. Now she was using her fingers to gain information and was fascinated by the sandpaper letters; she began to learn the sounds of the alphabet through her own interest in the letters.

Art, in particular, began to interest her. She often repeated an art lesson in class and liked lessons using balls of tissue paper and colored sawdust glued on paper. She copied her name for the first time during an art lesson. Using a pencil became a less difficult task.

At ten, Christina is now learning to read and can write her lessons in a workbook. She is in the transitional class and is learning at a slow but steady pace.

SPECIFIC LEARNING DISABILITIES

(Difficulties in one or more of the following: reading, writing, spelling, arithmetic. Academic failure. Example: A child may be able to read at a college level and yet be unable to spell well consistently. A child may be unable to read without great effort and yet can memorize math facts with ease.)

Case History

Andrew, age sixteen, was enrolled in one of the upper classes of a special school for learning disabilities. Although he had an excellent teacher and was doing well in reading, composition, and other academic subjects, he could not learn the simplest math concepts.

Testing revealed average intelligence but difficulties in seeing the relationship between objects and himself (spatial relations) and in understanding what he heard (auditory association or integration).

Andrew's teacher, aware of the excellent Montessori math materials, asked the teacher of the Montessori class for suggestions. As they talked, they realized that Andrew needed to start at the beginning of the Montessori math curriculum. They decided to invite Andrew to tutor the younger children in the Montessori class. Andrew was delighted. He came two mornings a week. The teacher demonstrated to him the material he was to teach, allowed him to practice, and then gave him a child to teach. Soon Andrew was a welcome aide in the classroom. The younger children liked him and learned from him.

As the school year went on, it became apparent that Andrew was learning math for the first time. Through his work with the manipulable materials, he could see and touch the concepts that had been so elusive in textbooks and on blackboards. His trouble seeing the relationship between objects and how parts of objects fit together cleared up. Understanding how spaces fit together is a skill basic to understanding how quantities or numbers relate to each other. Now math was not such a mystery. His teacher was amazed at his progress. Andrew is considering becoming a teacher.

CONCEPTUAL SKILLS

(The ability to think, to reason, and to understand concepts. Example: The child understands number facts and operations, has general information, and can classify and comprehend facts he knows and experiences he has had. On the basis of what he has learned in the past, the child is able to predict what may happen in the present and the future.)

Case History

Scott, age ten, had learning disabilities revolving around seeing the things around him correctly and understanding what he saw. His progress in reading was slow. He had trouble using his hands and eyes together in tasks like handwriting.

Psychological testing indicated he was functioning at the dull-normal range of intelligence and that he was immature, dependent, and learned best using concrete and manipulable materials. He was functioning on the first-grade level in reading and the second-grade level in mathematics.

Scott was placed in a self-contained Montessori class of less than ten children. It was soon clear that he liked using the materials in class. He liked using the geography equipment, especially the puzzle-maps and pictures of people living in other countries. He became curious about other ways of life and began to do his work in class quickly so as to get to the library and the *National Geographic* magazines.

Through his work with concrete materials, including the puzzle-maps of the continents, Scott could conceptualize the idea of different life-styles around the world. This ability allowed him to draw inferences in other academic areas as well.

There are many discoveries to make in a Montessori classroom, many of which are left unexplained by the teacher so that the child can discover them for himself. Making these discoveries gives the child a happy and rewarding experience. He has learned or discovered something by himself, without being taught or shown. Usually when this type of discovery is made, it is shared joyfully with the others in the class. Sharing the accomplishment spurs all the children on to think and discover for themselves. Scott was pleased with himself when he discovered that all triangles have three sides even though they are not all the same shape. He soon discovered that doors are rectangles and that feathers are common to all birds. He started to think. His joy in learning led to a better level in reading and math.

SOCIAL RELATIONSHIPS

(The ability to obey the rules of the classroom and society, to get along with other children and adults, to anticipate the outcome of actions, and to assume responsibility for oneself, others, and the environment. Example: Child is able to make and maintain friendships. He can play games with others in a fair and positive manner. He can think ahead to how his actions and words will affect others. He learns to think of others as well as himself and is helpful and considerate. He is well behaved.)

Case History

Kevin, age four, came to the adapted Montessori class after being asked to leave two nursery schools. He was badly behaved and unable to conform to the rules. He would not join group activities; he hit other children, and did not follow the teacher's directions. He was unhappy and angry and was a constant disturbance in class. His mother tried keeping him home for a time, but found that his behavior was beyond her control and that she needed help.

The pediatrician agreed that Kevin was hyperactive and, at the parents' request, prescribed medication. Psychological testing revealed a bright little boy.

Kevin hated the Montessori class. He cried the minute his mother left and refused to be comforted. His mother believed he was angry that he had to leave his old school and regarded this special school as punishment. Sometimes it would be a half-hour before he calmed down enough to allow the teacher or aide to approach him with something they hoped would attract his interest. This went on for about a week and, of course, bothered everyone in the classroom. Then one day the teacher's twelve-year-old daughter visited the class. Kevin allowed her to talk to him, and soon they were working together like old friends. He began to smile and enjoy the class for the first time.

Once Kevin decided the class was a fairly good place, he responded well to the ground rules. He learned he must not hit or disturb anyone else, and, even better, no one would disturb him. Once his behavior was more in control, he worked through the equipment quickly and wanted to learn more. He had good control over his body. He could kick a ball, run fast, jump in flips on the trampoline, and climb the highest playground equipment. He could speak in complete sentences, ask well thought-out questions, sing songs, and volunteer information.

He became the model for the other children. Instead of being the bad boy in class, he now regarded himself as a worthwhile person. He was able to recognize which of his actions were considered good and which were not. He was able to think before he acted. He still was mischievous but reponded well to correction. As his self-confidence increased, he was able to get along with his little sister and the neighborhood children. His mother reported that she could even take him visiting now because his behavior had improved.

Kevin was still hyperactive, but medication and structure kept this under control. Adults around him rewarded him for good behavior and tried to ignore the unacceptable. When situations became too much for him to handle, he was told to sit quietly until he could calm down. Later Kevin started to remove himself from the room when he needed to get into control. He became more responsible for his own actions.

In class, Kevin now welcomed new students and adult observers and proudly announced the rules. He was well-spoken, bright, charming, and kind and helpful to his classmates. He has graduated to a reguar kindergarten class, where he continues to lead others and to learn easily.

EMOTIONAL ADJUSTMENT

(The ability to accept oneself as a worthwhile human being who can take care of one's own needs. Example: Child is generally happy. He can accept change and enjoys a challenge. He is usually successful but can accept his mistakes. He is independent and does not cling to adults or need their continual approval.)

Case History

Maria's teacher came to a special school to inquire about admission. Maria, age nine, was a lovely girl who simply was not learning. She was not badly behaved, but she often withdrew into a fantasy world. Often she appeared to be frightened of the other children, new situations, and schoolwork. She clung to the teacher as much as she could. Afraid to try, she continually failed to perform as well as she could.

A psychological evaluation indicated inconsistent learning abilities because of emotional immaturity and anxiety. She was afraid to try because she was worried she would fail. This fear had interfered with her learning. It seemed to be a vicious circle: The more difficulty she had learning, the more uncertain she became; and the more uncertain she became, the more difficulty she had learning. Maria had stopped trying. Her parents and teacher were quite worried.

Maria was placed in a special Montessori class. She was not pressured to participate. At first, she was content to watch the teacher and the other children partake in the class activities. As Maria watched, she learned without having to perform and possibly fail. Tentatively she tried a few tasks. The teacher observed unnoticed and did not comment. Maria needed the freedom to make mistakes. The control of error in the Montessori equipment let her know if she was correct or not.

At first, Maria did not join the others on the playground. She preferred to be next to the teacher or near a wall. She seemed afraid of the other children. As time went on, she began to feel safer and joined in structured games led by the teacher. On field trips, she progressed from needing to hold the teacher's hand to being with a special girl friend.

When Maria gained in confidence, the teacher was able to present simple formal lessons. Maria was interested in the real materials around her. Choosing her work at certain times during the day gave her a feeling of being in control of herself. She gained independence and clung less to the teacher. Her interest grew, and she became less fearful because she was starting to have success. Aware that she was learning, she became less dependent on the teacher's approval.

After two years, Maria had outgrown her need for the structure and protection of the special school. She had started to participate in class, laugh easily, and try new assignments. Maria has returned to public school in her neighborhood. She is still a year behind academically, but is usually self-confident and happy. The little girl who used to hug the playground wall is now the terror of the community soccer team.

DEVELOPMENTAL DELAY

(Inconsistent and uneven development in movement, speech, and independence. This term is usually applied to a child who is too young to score consistently on standardized psychological tests and/ or eludes medical diagnosis. It is not known if the child is mentally retarded, emotionally disturbed, or learning-disabled. In this case, it is best to describe and treat the symptoms rather than misdiagnose or unfairly label the child. Example: A preschool child who can recite television commercials but who cannot tell adults his name. At the age of five or six, he needs help with toileting and washing his hands but can count to one hundred by fives. He cannot run, he cannot name the color red, but he knows the names of the letters of the alphabet and can draw circles. Diagnosticians rarely agree on the basic problem and its solution. They do agree that observation and careful teaching are the best approach.)

Case History

Anthony was almost four when he entered a Montessori preschool class of six children. He could not walk at a pace normal for a child his age. He had not walked until the age of three and still walked carefully with his feet wide apart. He could not follow even the simplest direction. When the teacher asked him to come sit on the floor with the other children, she had to take him by the hand, bring him to the group, and help him sit down. She placed Anthony next to her to insure that he would continue sitting with the group and not wander away.

Although he could form words, he did not use them to communicate with others. Instead he used gestures. He was hyperactive and had unreasonable fears and temper tantrums. In spite of all this, he liked music and stories and could recognize numbers.

Although Anthony was in the care of a psychiatrist, no clear diagnosis could be made. Psychological testing could not be done since he could not score on any of the standard tests. To label the child retarded, emotionally disturbed, or brain damaged would have been inaccurate and unfair.

Anthony was given a structured environment and consistent, supportive relationships with the adults in the environment. All instructions had to be given individually. He had a teacher to himself most of the time.

The support staff joined in. Anthony was given speech therapy twice a week to encourage him to use language as communication. Answering questions in words and then phrases and complete sentences was taught slowly and carefully. Naming exercises, which gave him a vocabulary, were given in class. The librarian found books on his level and read them to him. The psychologist observed him regularly and gave him individual play therapy when possible. The gross-motor specialist encouraged him to run, walk a balance beam, jump on a trampoline, catch a ball. The art teacher planned simplified lessons to insure success. The learning-disability specialist offered advice and coordinated the conferences of all those working with him.

As a result of this expertise and care, Anthony's concerned and patient parents reported that he was starting to speak about real things and events and sometimes even started conversation. He went out into the neighborhood playground and was accepted by some of the younger children in their play. He was starting to be good at climbing up and going down the slide. The parents were able to entertain other families with young children and not be embarrassed by Anthony's behavior.

In the past two years, Anthony has made limited progress. He can now follow directions and do some independent work. He is beginning to blend sounds into words. He enjoys the company of the other children and can dress and wash himself. He can run and jump well. Speech and response to conversation have improved.

Anthony still remains undiagnosed. His ability to learn indicates that he is not mentally retarded. Rather than giving him a label, the professionals and his parents are observing his needs and planning lessons and opportunities for growth to meet those needs.

SECTION THREE

Applications and Adaptations of Montessori for the Learning-Disabled Child

8. Montessori from a School Psychologist's Point of View

By Betsy Anderson

Working as a school psychologist with a Montessori Primary Unit has convinced me that the Montessori philosophy and teaching techniques are ideally suited to the emotional and learning needs of the learning-disabled and emotionally disturbed child. All children need a structured environment that provides opportunities for them to be able to work to their potential. This is especially true for those children whose perception of themselves and of their world has been fragmented and distorted by organic or emotional factors. Because of learning disabilities and emotional disturbances, these children have not been able to gather correct information from their environment by the full use of their senses. They have not had academic success and have not been able to master their environment or feel happy about themselves.

The following characteristics of the Montessori program, validated by the scientific observations of experts in the child-development field, provide these children with an atmosphere in which they can acquire the ego strength, or self-concept, necessary to cope successfully with their world.

Programmed Success. Since most of the emotionally disturbed and learning-disabled youngsters observed in the Montessori setting have experienced failure in their former schools and in their relationships with others, it is a heartwarming experience to see the timid, the angry, or the withdrawn child respond to a program designed for control of error, which lies in the material itself. This built-in control of error frees the child from constant correction by adults and allows him to learn and correct his own mistakes. As their talents unfold, their flagging self-images are strengthened, which produces a positive snowballing effect, leading finally to self-direction and self-control.

External Order. For the children who are disordered emotionally or perceptually, the Montessori method provides a prepared environment that remains reassuringly the same day after day. Gradually the children internalize the order provided by the classroom, thereby gaining mastery first over their environment and then over themselves.

Provisions for Reality Testing. Because of the small class size and the programmed materials, the teacher in a Montessori unit is able to be a psychologist-observer. She is free to help the child understand that rewards and consequences are a direct result of his behavior. She can help the child clarify in his own mind the reasons for his actions and encourage him to develop more productive behavior.

Opportunities for a Variety of Social Relationships. The Montessori classroom provides a wide opportunity for social experiences. There is adult guidance but no adult interference. The child has the opportunity for several levels of social interaction within the usual three-year age span in the classroom. He may choose to work alone; he may watch another child; he may work next to another child; or he may choose to work with one child or a group of children. Children may join together in a task, ask questions, enter into discussions. The classroom resembles an adult society with freedom of movement and choice of work and friends, but within rules for the common good. The child progresses from considering only himself to respecting and considering the rights of others as well.

Freedom of Choice. The Montessori environment also provides the most fundamental building block to decision making—freedom of choice in selecting from a wide variety of materials graded in difficulty and complexity.

In sum, the scientifically based Montessori approach to teaching helps the hurt, the damaged, and the ego-shattered child rebuild his personality in a controlled atmosphere and provides opportunities for successful achievement, emotional and social decision making, growth, and reality testing.

9. How to Use Montessori with Learning-Disabled Children

How do you do this? Why are these children learning? Why aren't they fighting? These children don't have very severe problems, do they? Why is it so peaceful and happy in this building? These are questions asked after people visit the Montessori Primary Unit at Leary School. They cannot understand why the children are happy and why they are learning when they have been so unsuccessful in their previous schools.

Maria Montessori must have been asked similar questions when educators observed her first schools. The answer is that the children are being taught according to the Montessori philosophy, the central point of which is that their needs are being met by the prepared environment and the curriculum and adults within that environment.

Importance of the Environment

At Leary School, the classrooms are immediately distinguishable from many other classrooms for learning-disabled children by the clean, attractive, orderly, and inviting atmosphere.

There are white child-sized shelves about the room on which the materials are displayed in sequential order. The boxes are kept in good repair, and the materials inside are checked continually by the teacher for completeness and order. Each piece of apparatus has its own place on the shelf. Things are not piled haphazardly on each other in broken boxes.

The learning materials are treated with great respect by both teachers and students. The Montessori materials are six years old and still in excellent condition.

The furniture in the classrooms is child-sized and movable. The three-to-six-year-old class is furnished with small tables and chairs. The classes for older children are furnished with movable school desks and brightly colored chairs.

When the Montessori Unit was started, the children moved their desks so that they faced a wall. It was clear that they were expressing their need for a quiet, undistracting place to work. The staff bought two-by-four-foot plywood sheets, shellacked them, and placed them between the desks, making study carrels or "offices." These boards are light and can be moved easily when two children want to work together at their desks.

In the rooms for the older children, there is also a large hexagonal table composed of two trapezoids. Here children come to work next to each other or together. Here also the teacher gives group lessons and can easily monitor the activities of several children at once. The children may choose to work on the floor on individual mats about two by four feet in size. The mat delineates the child's work space and allows the freedom of movement he needs.

There is no teacher's desk in a Montessori classroom. The teacher moves about, quietly giving lessons. The teachers store their records in a file cabinet and keep extra materials in a closed closet.

There are a few well-chosen pictures and posters on the wall at a child's eye level. Visual distractions such as mobiles and complex bulletin-board displays are avoided. Carpeting helps eliminate auditory distractions. There are child-sized sinks for self-care and practical life activities in the classrooms. Bathrooms are close by. There is a quiet place for the children to go to calm down when they are upset.

When you enter the Leary modified Montessori environment, you see children working at various tasks at desks, tables, or on the floor. There is quiet talk and purposeful movement. The teacher is aware of each child and gives him only the help he needs to succeed.

How does this differ from a regular Montessori class? The following outline shows how the Leary School has modified the Montessori environment and approach for its learning-disabled youngsters.

DIFFERENCES BETWEEN A REGULAR PRIMARY MONTESSORI CLASS AND A MONTESSORI CLASS MODIFIED FOR CHILDREN WITH LEARNING DISABILITIES

Class Size

Regular: twenty-five to thirty children taught by a teacher and an aide.
Modified: eight to ten children taught by a teacher and an aide.

Age Grouping

Regular: children ages two and one-half to six.
Modified: children ages three to six, six to eight, seven to nine, eight to thirteen, thirteen to seventeen, placed according to social and academic abilities.

Curriculum Materials

Regular: Montessori materials to prepare the child in the areas of practical life, sensory development, language, mathematics, history, art, music.
Modified: Montessori materials as above, as well as other materials to strengthen specific learning abilities and skills (Developmental Learning Materials, Peabody Language Kits, Gillingham, Frostig, Controlled Reader). Materials to introduce the children to public school work such as textbooks and workbooks.

Environment

Regular: Rich and varied. Large classroom. Movement and activity.
Modified: Smaller classroom. Fewer materials displayed. Quiet places to work without distraction.

Admission Process

Regular: Parent and child visit the school. Teacher becomes acquainted with the child.

Modified: Includes compiling of previous testing and school records. In-depth interview with the parent. Testing of child to determine intellectual level, academic achievement, learning abilities and disabilities, and emotional functioning. Medical examinations, including a vision and hearing screening. Psychiatric and/or neurological referral may be made.

Teaching Strategy

Regular: Teacher observes child, gives lessons, encourages choice and independence. When the child is successful in one step of the curriculum, he is introduced to the next.

Modified: Teacher observes child, studies records and test results. In conference with the parent, she plans the annual goals for the child's progress. She continues to observe, diagnose, and give lessons necessary to the child's progress, using the child's learning strengths. As the child starts to feel confident, she encourages choices and independence.

Learning Process

Regular: Child learns through his own experience with Montessori materials. Work with his hands with concrete objects leads to discoveries and thinking.

Modified: Child learns in the same manner.

Structure

Regular: Clear rules of conduct in the classroom lead to freedom of choice, movement, conversation.

Modified: Clear structure gives comfort. Child needs to know that his rights will be protected and that he is obligated to follow the rules. Freedom of choice, movement, and conversation evolve.

Individualization

Regular: Intrinsic in the Montessori approach. Each child learns at his own rate. Children learn from each other as well as from the teacher. Formal lessons may be given to an individual, group or class.

Modified: Lessons are individualized for each child's learning abilities and levels just as in the regular classroom. Individualization is even more important to learning-disabled children, who usually have uneven learning abilities and several levels of achievement (e.g., third-grade math, primer-level reading, sixth-grade science). Therefore the teacher must plan individual lessons for each child in her class.

As the child is ready, he is taught some subject matter, such as history in the form of stories read aloud by the teacher, in a group setting to aid his eventual return to a more regular class setting.

Choice

Regular: Choice leads to interest which leads to increased attention span, repetition, mastery, success, and concentration.

Modified: The same principle applies. To aid in the development of concentration, some children will need access to a quiet place to work.

Teacher Preparation

Regular: The teacher is Montessori trained and certified.

Modified: The teacher has a year of graduate Montessori training, experience in a regular Montessori classroom, and graduate work or in-service training in teaching learning-disabled children.

METHODS OF USING MONTESSORI WITH THE LEARNING-DISABLED CHILD

Tutoring: one-to-one, after school, using Montessori to teach or remediate specific skills or subjects

Resource Room: environment within a school to which students needing specific help are referred

Transitional Class: classroom using primarily traditional materials, but relying on Montessori methods for academic remediation and skill building

Special Montessori Class: classroom adaptation and simplification of the Montessori environment and curriculum for the child with special needs (eight to twelve students)

Regular Montessori School: may enroll a few children who need special help but who are not distracted by the movement and stimuli of a class of twenty-five to thirty-five children.

10. Outline of Adapted Montessori Curriculum for the Learning-Disabled Child

By Janet Fairbank

The curriculum in my Montessori class falls into the four basic areas of the traditional Montessori class: practical life, sensorial, language, and math exercises. Also included are geography, science, biology, music, rhythm and movement.

PRACTICAL LIFE EXERCISES

The practical life exercises have many learning purposes in a Montessori class: care of the environment, the need for order in the environment, fine and gross motor coordination, independence, sequencing, care of self, left-to-right movement in individual tasks, and building concentration.

The practical life exercises which promote all of the above include:

Care of Environment

pouring rice	develop fine motor control
	make child aware of the neatness of an action
pouring water	foster independence
washing a table	a task requiring more than 50 steps in sequencing

polishing a mirror
polishing silver   } sequencing
watering plants   } fine motor control
dusting
woodworking and painting }

Care of Self

dressing frames:
  buttons   } independence
  zipper   } fine motor control
  snaps   } sequencing
  tying   } visual motor skills
  lacing

Other practical life activities include cutting; peeling carrots; setting the table at lunchtime with placemats, napkins, and straws; and sponging off one's place at the end of the meal. Responsibility for the general order and cleanliness of the classroom is shared among the students. In particular, the return of materials to the proper place by each student is encouraged.

SENSORIAL EXPERIENCES

The aim of the sensorial materials and exercises is to aid the child in the process of classification within and orientation to his environment. The sensorial materials offer the child experiences from which he is able to draw abstract knowledge. This manipulable equipment encourages movement, both fine and gross motor, and utilizes the child's visual, auditory, tactile, and kinesthetic senses as he deals with sound, color, size, texture, quantity, and shape. With these materials, the child manipulates, pairs, grades, compares, and matches, drawing his own conclusions according to his level of abilities and perceptions.

The sensorial materials and exercises in my class include:

Sense of Sight and Size Discrimination

Solid cylinders—four blocks containing ten knobbed cylinders of different dimensions, each fitting into its own hole.

Pink tower—ten cubes differing in length, breadth, and height. Their sizes grow progressively in the algebraic series of the third power.

Brown stairs—ten brown prisms of the same length, differing in breadth and height.

Red rods—ten red rods differing in length.

Binomial and trinomial cubes—wooden cubes and rectangular prisms, painted various colors. One box contains pieces forming a cube of $(a + b + c)^3$. The child learns to take these apart and reassemble them.

All of the above concern the child's sense of visual discrimination, gross and fine motor control.

Color Discrimination

First color box—a box containing three pairs of small tablets, each pair painted one of the primary colors. Child matches and learns names of the colors.

Second color box—a box containing twenty-two tablets of secondary colors.

Third color box—a box with nine compartments, each containing seven tablets in shades of a single color. Child grades these colors from dark to light.

The above materials and exercises develop the child's sense of color.

Stereognostic and Sight Senses

Geometric solids—different geometric forms: sphere, oval, ellipsoid, cube, rectangular prism, square, pyramid, ovoid. The child learns to recognize these forms blindfolded and learns the corresponding names.

Geometric cabinet—a cabinet of six drawers containing six figures each, including circles, triangles, rectangles, polygons, and so on. The child participates in exercises of varying difficulty, including matching, tracing, and learning the corresponding names of shapes. These exercises help the child in visual and muscular discrimination of form and indirectly prepare him for writing from left to right.

Knobless cylinders—these are the same as the solid cylinders, but without knobs; each set is a different color, and they are contained in boxes. They teach size discrimination.

Constructive triangles—four boxes: a triangular box, a large hexagonal box, a smaller hexagonal box, a rectangular box—all containing various kinds, sizes, and colors of triangles, some with black lines on one, two, or three sides, which the child matches and pairs to make new and different triangles and geometric shapes. These exercises give practical experience in plane geometry.

Tactile Sense

Rough and smooth touch boards—two boards divided into graded sandpaper and smooth wood which the child feels and describes.

Rough and smooth touch tablets—six pairs of tablets varying in surface texture of sandpaper. Child is blindfolded and asked to match the pairs (after proper preparation). These materials develop the tactile sense and indirectly prepare the child for writing.

Stereognostic Sense

Mystery bag—child is blindfolded and must identify objects inside a bag by touch alone.

Progressive exercises—child is blindfolded and must regroup and match buttons of several different sizes and shapes using only his hands.

Auditory Sense

Sound boxes—two paired boxes, each containing six cylinders, each of which contains a different quantity of beads or other materials so that every one makes a different sound when it is shaken. The child must mix the cylinders, then pair them, and then grade them according to sound produced, from loud to soft.

Non-Montessori Materials and Exercises

Non-Montessori materials and exercises used to extend work in the Sensorial area to continue the development of fine-motor skills and visual discrimination are:

Inch cubes and pattern cards—colored cubes and one-inch cards printed with increasingly difficult patterns made from one-inch squares. Child builds patterns with cubes first on and then off the cards.

Parquetry blocks and pattern cards—colored blocks in the shape of squares, triangles, and diamonds, and cards printed with increasingly difficult patterns made from the same shapes. Child uses these as he uses the inch cubes, though these designs are more advanced.

Pegboard and pattern cards—box of colored plastic pegs, a 6" x 6" plastic pegboard, and cards with patterns of increasing difficulty. Child copies patterns on board with pegs.

Other materials and activities

Simple large puzzles with knobs—child uses fingers to grasp knob in order to remove and replace puzzle piece.

Large kindergarten blocks—child builds structures.

Clay—child uses hands to build objects.

Tinker Toys—child builds more complicated structures.

Clothespins and cigar box—child uses his fingers to pinch clothespins and place around the rim of the cigar box.

Food color, water, and small bowl—child squeezes bags of food color into bowls of water and discovers how colors blend.

Large beads and string—child strings the beads according to his own design or in following a pattern.

Pegboard with large pegs—child places pegs in a board according to his own design or teacher's instructions.

Assorted sizes of nuts and bolts and a small basket—child twists bolts off the nuts and mixes them up. He then rejoins the nuts and bolts according to correct size.

Small bottles of various sizes and shapes in a basket—child twists off the lids from bottles, mixes them up, and replaces them.

All of the above promote fine motor control and visual-motor abilities and lend themselves to socialization. Some of the materials lead to work with the more demanding Montessori materials and some provide more repetition of a skill introduced by the Montessori curriculum.

LANGUAGE

The language program in my Montessori class consists of:

1. development of vocabulary, spoken expression, clarity of speech
2. writing
3. recognition of written symbols: reading

Enrichment of vocabulary, self-expression, presented through

discussions
stories read aloud and discussed
group singing, finger plays
classification of environment—naming objects
Peabody Language Development Kit—commercially produced kit containing puppets, records, and pictures in various categories (food, clothing, toys, animals, etc.) designed to build vocabulary and encourage language skills. Found to be a useful supplement

oral games to build auditory memory, in which the child is given increasingly complicated directions to follow, such as "Stand on one foot. Pat your head. Touch your left elbow."

The children are encouraged to participate in class discussions and to respect each other's opinions and feelings. They are discouraged from interrupting each other. They are encouraged to raise their hands and to talk softly.

Writing

Indirect Preparation includes the following:

1. solid cylinders (develops pincer grip in preparation for holding a pencil, fine motor control)
2. tactile exercises (sandpaper tablets—grading and matching)
3. geometry cabinet (develops pincer grip, left-right movement)
4. pegboards, finger exercises, games—Tinkertoy, pickup sticks, jacks (pincer grip, left-right)
5. art activities—projects such as paper tearing and pasting, building sculptures with small pieces of styrofoam and toothpicks, macramé, God's eyes, painting, and printing all stress fine-motor and visual-motor skills

Direct Preparation includes the following:

1. Sandpaper letters—these employ the child's auditory, kinesthetic, visual, and tactile senses. Contrasting shapes and sounds are presented through the Three-Period Lesson, a lesson designed to teach names and qualities such as color and size (this lesson is explained fully on pages 126-128). Phonetic sounds of the letters—not their names—and short vowel sounds are taught.
2. Movable alphabet (introduced when child has learned enough sandpaper letters to make a few words)—isolate sounds the child knows from whole alphabet and give the child three-letter phonetic words, a letter at a time. We don't ask child to read them back. The child continues working with the sandpaper letters over the weeks until he has learned the whole alphabet. When he is ready, he is encouraged to read the words back. He may not be ready to read his words back for months. The child then matches the written word on a card with those he has composed with the movable alphabet. The child writes three-letter phonetic, four-letter phonetic, and multisyllabic phonetic words (*mom, jet, unit, magnet, pigpen, zigzag*, etc.).

Forming Letters

Metal Insets: The child traces around metal shapes in left-right direction and colors them left-right as preparation for writing in the left-to-right sequence. As the child gains in control, more complex metal insets are introduced. The insets are superimposed on each other to form designs and extend interest.

Sand: The child makes letters in sand tray with his fingers.

Clay: The child rolls clay into a long cylinder and forms letters with it, thus building up his fine motor control and ability to form and recognize letters.

Vertical surfaces: Child writes and draws on a chalkboard or an opaque-polished window or mirror.

Horizontal surfaces: Child writes at a desk on a small blackboard, first on a blank blackboard, then on a lined blackboard. Subsequently he writes on unlined and then lined paper with progressively narrower lines.

Experiental writing: Child draws a picture of something that has happened or of a story he has imagined, and writes the story of the picture himself or dictates it to the teacher. This can develop into writing and illustrating booklets.

Reading (after child had learned to write with movable alphabet)

Phonetic Object Game: Given miniature objects representing phonetic words (such as *hat, pig, man, clip*), the child matches them to the words written on slips of paper. He realizes the written word is a symbol for the object. Phonetic words follow the standard sounds of the alphabet and have short vowels. They can be read easily by saying the sounds of the letters and then blending them into a word.

Phonetic Reading Cards: The child reads three-letter phonetic reading cards aloud. After proficiency here, he goes to four-letter words and beyond, e.g., *mat, jump, dentist.*

The child is introduced to simple, short, phonetic readers which can be read in one sitting. The child is encouraged to read aloud.

Phonograms (words in which two adjoining sounds blend or change into another sound, e.g., *sh, ph.*)

1. Phonogram object box—the child matches miniature objects to words written on slips of paper. One word has a phonogram in it, for example, *ship*, which introduces the sound *sh*.

2. Small movable alphabets—child composes words using two small alphabets, each of a different color, each stored in its own

box. One color is used for the phonogram, the other for the rest of the word. This isolates the phonogram and makes it easier to recognize and learn.

3. Phonogram booklets—child reads small book that has one word of a set of phonograms (*shop, shut, shed*) written on each page.

4. Phonogram cards—child reads a 5" x 8" card on which is printed a set of phonogram words. There are about thirty such cards.

Puzzle words: Words that follow no rules (*the, because, said*) are a puzzle and have to be memorized through the Three-Period Lesson of Seguin (see Chapter 14, How to Give a Montessori Lesson).

Reading Labels: The child places appropriate labels on objects in the classroom (*sink, door, map, stand, geometry cabinet*). He matches, pairs, and reads labels on language cards (3" x 5" picture-cards) showing birds, mammals, automobiles, composers, presidents of the United States.

The child is introduced to texts and workbooks he is likely to use in his next school.

MATHEMATICS

Math in a Montessori class includes exploration, movement, repetition, and sequencing activities and gives the child possibilities of making abstractions from concrete experiences.

For teaching the mathematical concepts involved in various Montessori materials, the following preparation is used:

Numbers 0–9

1. Quantity. Number rods—ten wooden rods in graded lengths, colored red and blue in alternate sections, each section being a decimeter in length and representing one number on the rod. The child learns the names of the numbers and makes the association between the correct number and the quantity 1–10.

2. Symbol. Sandpaper numbers—a set of numerals from 1 to 9 cut out of sandpaper and mounted on separate cards. The child

learns the symbols representing the quantity he already knows and is prepared for writing numbers.

3. Quantity and Symbol.

a. Number rods and cards—the number rods and a set of cards on which are printed the numbers 1 to 10. The child associates the written symbol, the number, with the quantity as represented by the rod.

b. Spindle boxes—two boxes, each divided into five compartments; at the back of each compartment is painted one of the numbers 0 to 9 in sequence. Forty-five spindles in a basket or box. The child makes sets by placing the appropriate numbers of spindles in each compartment. Introduction of zero—it gets no spindles.

c. Numbers and counters—numbers 1 to 10, cut from wood, and fifty-five counters of one color in a box. The child recognizes numbers 1 to 10 and sequences them correctly. Counters placed in pairs under numbers give a visual representation of odd and even numbers because there is one counter left over in the odd numbers while the even numbers pair up evenly.

d. Number memory game—numbers 1 to 10 written on separate pieces of paper. Child chooses a number and looks about the classroom for that number of objects, e.g., 6 cotton balls, 7 triangles. Makes children realize that numbers are useful and strengthens memory.

Teens

1. Quantity. Teen beads—nine bars of ten golden beads each and nine bead bars in different colors representing quantities 1–9. Child learns to make and count numbers 11–19 with a 10-bar and a colored-bead bar. For example, 11 is represented by a 10-bar and a bar of one red bead and 15 is represented by a 10-bar and a bar of 5 blue beads.

2. Symbol. Teen board—a number frame divided into nine spaces in each of which is written the number 10. Child is provided with wooden slats numbered 1–9 and slots them into the spaces, making the numerals 11–19. Child thus learns to make and read the symbols for the quantities 11–19.

3. Quantity and Symbol. Teen board and beads—materials as

above. Child counts beads and places the correct quantity next to the number on the board and so learns to connect symbol and quantity.

Tens

Bead chains hung in a frame so as to represent the squared and cubed quantities of 1–10. Labels on each chain connect quantity and symbol. Child learns to skip count using the bead chains, touching and labeling chains up to 1000 beads.

Decimal System

1. Quantity. Beads—set of beads representing units in single beads, tens in bars of ten beads, hundreds in squares of one hundred beads, and thousands in cubes of one thousand beads. Child learns the quantity by holding and feeling the weight of the various quantities and by seeing the quantities represented in the beads.

2. Symbol. Cards—box containing four sets of cards with numerals written on them. Units from 1–9 written in green. Tens from 10–90 written in blue. Hundreds from 100–900 written in red. Thousands from 1000–9000 written in green. Child learns the names and how to read the numbers representing the quantities he has learned with the beads.

3. Quantity and Symbol. Beads and cards—set of beads and cards like 2 above, showing thousands. Child learns to read numbers and matches them to the corresponding quantity in the beads.

Mathematical Operations:
Addition, subtraction, multiplication and division

1. Introduction. Beads and cards—set of decimal system beads and cards. Group of three or four children learns that combining beads is called addition, that taking away beads is called subtraction, that adding the same number several times is called multiplication, and that sharing out a quantity of beads is called division. While they practice with the beads, they match and read the number cards and also learn the symbols +, −, ×, and ÷ and their meanings.

2. Memorization of facts. A series of charts giving practice in memorization of facts in addition, subtraction, multiplication, and division. For each operation, there are small slips of folded paper on which problems are written. For example, in addition, $4 + 2 =$, $3 + 9 =$, $2 + 7 =$. The child looks up the answer on the chart and writes the problem and the answer. After doing a series of such problems, he checks his own work for accuracy on a Control Chart, which gives the addition tables. With time and practice, he memorizes the addition facts. This process is repeated for subtraction, multiplication, and division.

Non-Montessori materials used to further the work in the math area are:

discussion of the clock and calendar, of the passage and recording of time

games and chores such as counting classmates, setting the table for a certain number of people, taking only two cookies from the tray

worksheets to give practice in mathematical operations in a purely symbolic form.

textbooks used in the school the child is likely to enter later

OTHER CURRICULUM AREAS AND TEACHING MATERIALS

Geography

sandpaper globe
painted globe
puzzle-maps of world, continents, United States
continent envelope kits (each envelope deals with one continent and contains color-coded boards on which are mounted pictures of the peoples and countries of the continent)

History

pictures
stories
museum attendance

Science

nature walks
experiments conducted in class
stories and texts

Music

sound boxes
bells
songs, finger plays, rhythm games
appreciation by listening to recorded music, discussing composers, instruments, feelings while listening
concert attendance

Art

cutting
drawing
painting
skills leading to creativity such as method of holding brush, mixing colors, shading, picture composition
appreciation by looking at pictures of famous artists, discussing the pictures and the lives of the artists, choosing favorite pictures to hang in the classroom
visits to galleries

Movement

free play
climbing, running, skipping, jumping
directed gross motor activities:
1. balance beam—a wooden beam approximately six feet long and 2 inches by 4 inches in width along which a child walks to practice balance. May be raised off the floor.
2. rocker board—a board approximately 2 feet by 2 feet mounted on rockers. Child stands on it with legs apart, rocks and maintains balance.
3. ball on a string—a small ball suspended by a string from the

ceiling. Child hits the ball with a bat divided into colored sections, trying to make the hit with a particular section of the bat.

4. grid mat activities—a plastic mat six feet square with nine equal sections marked. Child plays hopping and stepping games by placing body in specified sections.

5. tumbling—tumbling mat. Child performs tumbling activities such as rolling, crawling, somersaults, cartwheels, handstands.

6. trampoline—Child sit-bounces, knee-bounces, stand-bounces, and moves into progressively more difficult activities.

Games

kick ball
soccer
basketball
softball
football

11. Montessori as Remediation; Use with Adolescents

Just as Montessori materials can be used to build academic skills for a young child who has none, they can also be used to improve the older child's ability to learn and raise his academic level.

TRANSITIONAL CLASS

For children who enter the Montessori Unit at Leary School with fairly good academic skills, the Montessori materials are used to correct specific weaknesses uncovered by testing and to ease difficulties encountered in texts and workbooks. For example, some children cannot memorize addition combinations, such as $3 + 5 = 8$ and $6 + 4 = 10$, even with much practice in workbooks and repeated explanations from the teacher. If they do not understand the quantitites being expressed in written symbols, work with paper and pencil causes confusion, frustration, and perhaps anger. Making the concept of addition concrete with the Montessori mathematics materials which they can touch, move, and see shows them how 3 plus 5 amounts to 8 and 6 plus 4 amounts to 10. Once they understand the concept behind the facts, they memorize the facts more easily.

It is considered best to use the traditional materials with which such children, are familiar from their previous schools and to introduce the sequenced Montessori materials where they are needed to reinforce one concept or another.

Older children often come to the younger classes as tutors, and while they are helping the young children, they build their own skills as well. These tutors become friends of the younger children, and several have discovered a genuine ability to teach.

RESOURCE ROOM

Montessori can also be used in a resource room to which children are referred from other classes because of a particular difficulty. The materials appeal to older children and teenagers as well as to young children.

Montessori was first introduced at Leary School as a resource program. The following is adapted from an article describing this program originally published in *Children's House* magazine.*

Approximately 20 percent of the two hundred students at Leary School have been referred to the Montessori Resource Room. Those accepted come in groups of three or four for two half-hour sessions per week to supplement their regular classroom programs. The age of the students ranges from seven to sixteen. We meet in a small, clean room with a large, rectangular table in the center and a small desk against the wall for the student who wishes to work on his own. On two walls are shelves on which the Montessori equipment is arranged in sequence of difficulty. The materials include those for sensorial education as well as for language and mathematics.

Usually students are referred to the Montessori program by their teachers or the director. Their difficulties with handwriting, spelling, or mathematics usually are caused by an extraordinary need to develop some particular basic perceptual or visual-motor ability. Math, for instance, depends on size discrimination, spatial relationships, laterality, dominance, sequencing, form perception, and so on.

*"Montessori and the Learning Disabled Child," Foster, Marjorie, *Children's House*, Vol. 8, No. 1 (Summer 1975): 6–11. © 1975 by Children's House, Inc. By permission of Children's House, Inc.

To determine the strong and weak areas and to plan a program before I work with a particular student, I study his record thoroughly, observe him in class, and confer with his teacher. I confer with the student also. Before he begins with a group, the student visits the Montessori Room. I explain the program to him briefly and show him how to do at least one task so that he can teach it to another student when his group begins. This interview also allows for additional diagnosing and planning. Most important, we discuss the reason he has been referred to the Montessori Room and what the probable program will be. The student is usually very aware of his problem and is eager to discuss it and its solution in a frank and open manner. Often this is the most enlightening aspect of the study I do of the student, and it begins to establish trust and rapport.

It is important to recognize that although a child may be twelve chronologically, he may have a much younger developmental level in some areas. For example, he may have the skills of a four-year-old in eye-hand coordination. Working with the Montessori equipment designed to develop eye-hand coordination will allow this child to improve in this respect and thereby to advance academically much more easily and quickly than before. Teachers and parents comment on the progress made by older children who have been helped in this way.

The students are grouped for the Montessori program according to their chronological ages and the areas needing improvement. Most lessons are given individually in a step-by-step demonstration of how to perform an exercise. After the student is proficient in the exercise, he may teach another student—something the children truly enjoy. Some take materials back to class to teach other children not included in the program.

One group of three, who range in age from eleven to thirteen, has severe learning disabilities. They have an excellent teacher thoroughly trained in teaching this type of child, and she has recognized the need for a systematic program using manipulable materials that will build perception, integration, and output skills. One boy in this group has difficulty interpreting what he sees and hears and using his hands and eyes together. Further, he is not sure if he is right-or left-handed. In just five months, he has moved from the solid cylinder blocks—a basic exercise in size discrimination, fine hand coordination, and problem-solving skills—to the multiplication bead board, a much more complex exercise. The board has one hundred indentations of ten across and ten down, representing the multiplication facts. By placing small beads in patterns in the indentations, the student sees and discovers multiplication tables. For instance, when the child places four beads across each of three rows he can count and see that he has made the fact $4 \times 3 = 12$. In this careful work with his hands, he is also building fine motor control and increasing his skill in using his eyes and hands together. This boy is extremely proud of his progress through the equipment. He is even prouder of his growing knowledge of multiplication tables and asks for harder and harder work in multiplication. Even though he is very distractible and sometimes difficult to manage, he concentrates and works with minimal supervision when occupied with the manipulable material.

The other two boys in this group are equally proud of their progress, although they have chosen a different direction in which to move. Currently one is very busy working on copying patterns from cards with pegs on a pegboard. He has pronounced difficulty with visual perception (seeing correctly) and with spatial relationships (knowing how spaces fit together), shown by his marked inability to copy words from a blackboard or read easily in a textbook. Working with the pegboard gives him an opportunity to build the learning abilities he needs to manage writing and reading. The third boy in this group has worked his way through the sensorial and the beginning math equipment and is now asking for help in his spelling, so next we will work with the sandpaper letters and movable alphabet.

A group of older students—twelve, thirteen, and fifteen—were referred for academic deficiencies. One of the boys, age thirteen, has great difficulty remembering math facts and operations. He has pronounced problems in form perception (is it a circle or a square?), size discrimination (which is bigger?), and spatial relationships (how does it fit together?). He has erratic work habits and does not always work from left to right. It is no wonder he has trouble with math. His math teacher, the student, and I had a frank discussion of his underlying difficulties and the best method to use for removing them. In math class, he concentrates on facts and processes, while in the Montessori Room, he concentrates on improving his basic visual-motor skills and work habits. This student sees that he is progressing and is now coming to work in the Montessori Room after school.

The twelve-year-old in this group was referred because of poor handwriting. A check in the records revealed visual-motor and perceptual distortion with superimposed emotional problems. Since he was having difficulty using his hands and eyes together, he could not write as well as his friends, which caused frustration and anger. Sometimes he behaved badly in class, and he had started to shun his friends. This boy knew how the letters looked, but not how they felt when he was writing them. He had to think how to form the letters each time he wrote something because he had no muscular memory of the formation of a letter. He learned the lower-case alphabet very quickly by tracing sandpaper letters and then writing the letters very large on the blackboard with his eyes averted. Now he brings in acceptable samples of handwriting from class in exchange for the privilege of working with the math equipment. We are still working on the upper-case alphabet.

The third boy in this group, age fifteen, was also referred for illegible handwriting. Although he is very intelligent and has much to communicate, he could not write down what he knew because of pronounced gross and fine motor and visual discrimination problems. Since he did not have control over the large muscles of his body and the small muscles of his hands, a task like writing was very difficult. This was further complicated by his not being able to correctly interpret information taken in by his eyes. He is in a special physical education class to increase body coordination while he works on hand coordination and visual skills in the Montessori room and in his regular class. Through practice with the sensorial equipment and sandpaper letters, this boy is now able to form the letters and has progressed to practicing letters on wide-lined red paper. His teacher, who is also working on his handwriting in her class, told me that he has turned in his first two-page written report.

The children are excited by discoveries they make with the materials. A boy working with the multiplication bead board suddenly exclaimed, "Oh, I see, you add three each time when you multiply by threes!" An eleven-year-old boy who had been working with the geometric solids looked about the room and said, "Hey we are inside a rectangular prism. All rooms are rectangular prisms!" and one child instructed another, "Put that cylinder on the table quietly. It's for fine hand coordination."

Even more important than the fact that the students like the materials and learn from them is how applicable the general theory of Montessori is to the overall education of the child with learning disabilities. During my work with these children I have made several observations.

1. Given freedom to choose their own activities within the structure of the environment, the children have been remarkably sensitive to their own needs. For example, those who have an academic weakness in math will choose the geometry cabinet and cards.

2. To master a skill, the students will repeat it over and over again, and need to be allowed to do so undisturbed. My records show that one boy with a severe spatial relationship problem, who often cried when his work was too hard, repeated the trinomial cube, a difficult three-dimensional puzzle, for five half-hour periods. Now that he has mastered it, he enthusiastically teaches it to others and is tackling more difficult work.

3. Working with the hands often calms an upset child. Last year one student often came into the room angry about something that had happened that day. He would usually choose the multiplication chart and work alone until he was in control of himself. Then he was ready to learn something new with me.

4. Abstract concept formation takes place as the child uses his senses in the manipulation of physical objects. Manipulation of concrete materials allows the child to learn through his own movements and experience. He becomes the active agent in his learning. He can touch language and mathematics himself. One girl once held the hundred-bead square in one hand and the thousand-bead cube in the other and said, "Now I feel the difference."

5. While the child is forming concepts with these materials, he is refining his perceptual and motor abilities. He is learning to see and hear correctly and to use his hands and eyes together. For instance, a student placing beads on the multiplication bead board with his thumb and fingers is discovering or conceptualizing his multiplication tables and at the same time performing a fine motor task.

6. The Montessori materials are an excellent diagnostic tool. For example, while observing a student work with the solid cylinders— ten cylinders of different sizes which he places in their proper holes—I can get a number of indications of his learning abilities. Work habits are revealed by where he places the cylinders on the table: all over the work surface or in front of the cylinder block where

he can reach them easily. Problem-solving abilities are indicated by his method of replacing the cylinders: by trial and error or by looking at the hole and finding the correct cylinder. Directional sequence is revealed if the child chooses to work left to right or right to left or in a random fashion. Fine motor control shows in the way the child grasps the cylinder with his thumb and fingers. Visual discrimination for size is indicated by the child's success in finding the correct hole for the cylinder on the first try.

7. Because the materials are designed to lead the child through a logical sequence of work which becomes increasingly difficult, he can start at his success level in the Montessori materials and know that mastery at one level will lead to mastery at the next. The students enjoy seeing where they began, where they are now, and where they are going.

8. The habit of success for children who were used to failure is especially important. Mastery of skills in the protected environment of the Montessori classroom builds self-confidence and leads to mastery in the environment of the regular classroom and in the larger environment outside the school.

9. Older children respond to the order and structure of the Montessori classroom just as younger children do. They respect the right of others to work undisturbed. Given structure, they treat the materials with respect and care and replace things where they belong on the shelves. From order, conceptualizations and good work habits develop. A twelve-year-old boy looked around the room one day and told me, "I love this room. It is so clean and everything is in order on the shelves. I feel secure in here."

12. How to Set Up a Montessori Classroom Environment

For a new, regular Montessori class of children aged three to six who will have a three-hour morning at school, the following steps will result in a well-functioning class. Start with only ten to twelve children and add more children (up to a total of twenty-five) gradually.

Before the children enter:

1. Empty the classroom of materials, furniture, wall decorations
    a. Paint the room a flat off-white
    b. Wash the windows
    c. An asphalt-tile floor in a pretty color is preferred
2. Obtain:
    a. low child-sized shelving painted with white enamel
    b. child-sized desks and/or small tables and chairs
    c. mats, about 2 feet by 3 feet, in bright colors that can be easily rolled for storage—for work sitting on the floor
    d. plants—for the children to water and watch grow
    e. a few art prints and/or posters for language development
    f. some simple, clear books with good illustrations for reading stories aloud

      g. a record player and records of classical music and children's songs

      h. selected Montessori equipment: pouring exercises, dusting cloths, mystery bag

      i. selected toys: large blocks, large wooden puzzles with knobs, clay

      j. a Montessori teacher and possibly an aide

   3. Know the children who will enter through:

      a. records—the admission file

      b. preschool interview by the teacher

After the children enter:

   1. Set the ground rules carefully to establish structure.

   2. At first, give most of the lessons to the children in groups. Include songs, art activities, stories, and outside play. Have how-to lessons such as how to have a snack, how to hang up a coat, how to walk around mats and roll them for storage, how to dust shelves.

   3. Introduce a short work period with children choosing toys to play with individually or in small groups.

   4. Start to introduce beginning Montessori equipment: pouring rice, pink tower, first color box.

   5. As time goes on, decrease time devoted to group lessons and increase work time when children choose tasks. Eventually in a three-hour morning, two to two and a half hours should be devoted to this individual work time.

   6. Continue to teach the use of Montessori equipment. As some of the children become familiar with the materials, place the equipment on the shelf. As time goes on, the children will become more interested in the Montessori equipment and less interested in the toys. Gradually remove the toys and introduce more Montessori equipment.

At first, the environment will look bare with only a few pieces of equipment on the shelves. When the children are able to make choices among tasks and to work independently, more materials can be introduced and displayed on the shelves. In June, the room will look very different from the way it looked in September.

For a new class adapting Montessori methods for children ages three to six, six to nine, or nine to twelve who have learning disabilities, start with five to six children and add more children (up to a total of eight or ten) gradually. The six-to-nine and nine-to-twelve groups will be in school the full day, while the three-to-six group will have only a three-hour morning.

Before the children enter:

1. Prepare the classroom as for the regular Montessori class, except that blue or green carpet is preferred as it reduces noise and distractions.

2. Obtain:

    a. shelving: low white shelves for the three-to-six and six-to-nine groups, higher shelves for the nine-to-twelve group

    b. child-sized tables and chairs for the three-to-six group; small desks and unattached chairs for the six-to-twelve group; movable partitions to place between two desks facing the wall to form "offices" for undistracting places to work; a large table for the center of the room for group work

    c. mats—even nine-to-twelve-year-olds like to work on floor

    d. plants

    e. limited visual distractions—only one or two prints or posters

    f. books on the level of the class in the areas of reading, math, science, history, geography, literature. At least one good book for reading a continuous story aloud to the six-to-twelves.

    g. a record player and records

    h. selected Montessori equipment

        (1) 3–6: beginning practical life and sensorial

        (2) 6–9: same as 3–6, but add puzzle maps of continents, United States, sandpaper letters

        (3) 9–12: same as 6–9, but add number rods, sandpaper numbers

    i. other selected equipment:

        (1) 3–6: toys as for regular class

        (2) 6–9: toys, but add reading books on level of children, paper, pencils, crayons

        (3) 9–12: games such as cards, dominoes, clay, paper,

pencils, workbooks, and books a bit below level of the children
  j. a teacher:
    (1) Montessori-trained, with special-education training
3. Specialists as needed:
  a. speech therapist
  b. psychologist
  c. motor specialist or physical-education teacher
  d. art teacher
  e. learning-disabilities consultant
  f. aide—to give even more individual attention
4. Know the children who will enter through:
  a. records, such as previous testing in academic achievement, learning abilities; intellectual level, emotional functioning, social and educational history
  b. preschool interview of parent and child by the teacher
After the children enter:
1. Set the ground rules for conduct clearly and carefully to establish structure for behavior.
2. Set the time frame of the day—write the activities and times on the board—to establish structure for time.
3. At first give most lessons in groups.
  a. 3–6: same as regular class, only repeat lessons often
  b. 6–9, 9–12: give individual work at the child's own desk, give traditional paper and pencil tasks in addition to group work of stories, songs, how-to lessons
4. Give a short work period (ten to fifteen minutes) with a choice of activities using the items on shelves. As the children become interested and can work for longer periods of time, still following the rules of conduct, the work time can be increased.
5. Start introducing the Montessori equipment for the teaching or reteaching of basic skills. Display it on shelving. Continue work in texts and workbooks for the nine-to-twelves and use the Montessori equipment to teach concepts and build skills necessary for success with paper and pencil. When the six-to-nines have learned concepts and skills with the Montessori equipment, introduce workbooks and texts.
6. Gradually increase work time to two hours in the morning and one hour in the afternoon. This allows for choice, interest,

development of attention span, concentration, and mastery. The child will become more independent and successful than if he is told what to do every minute of the day.

7. Include a specified time for language development (group lessons in following directions, verbal expression), motor development (teach basic movement and body awareness skills child may lack). Plan field trips, parties, and class plays when the children are ready.

8. Continue to observe, diagnose, and teach to the needs of the child.

By January or February, the new Montessori class adapted for children with learning disabilities will be a happy, productive place. People coming to observe will go away saying, "Why are these children here? There is nothing wrong with them."

13. Ground Rules of a Montessori Classroom, or How to Structure for Behavior

A non-Montessori teacher can utilize much of the philosophy and technique of the Montessori method in her teaching. For instance, the structure or ground rules of behavior can be applied in almost every form of teaching.

Based on the theory that outer discipline leads to internal discipline, structure is essential in a Montessori classroom.

The structure for behavior is set by the teacher and acts as a railing on a bridge. Within the structure, the child moves confidently. Without the structure, he is frightened and gropes for the limits of behavior. Therefore structure allows the child maximum individual freedom to learn, grow, and be happy.

As the child internalizes the structure, the teacher withdraws slowly. It is a Montessori principle that as the child increases in ability, the teacher decreases her influence.

The following ground rules for a Montessori classroom work equally well in a normal Montessori class and a class for children with learning disabilities, and can be used by non-Montessori teachers.

CARE AND USE OF THE MATERIALS

1. A child may choose a piece of equipment from the shelves and work with it as long as he wishes without being disturbed by others.

2. He must use the materials with respect. He may not abuse them. He is free to make discoveries and is encouraged to talk about what he has learned.

3. When he is finished, the child cleans the materials if necessary. He returns the equipment in good order to the correct place on the shelf, knowing that he is making it ready for the next child to use.

CARE AND USE OF THE ENVIRONMENT

1. A child may choose to work at his desk, at a table, or on a mat on the floor.

2. Children may not disturb the work of others or enter another's work space without invitation.

3. When he is finished, the child leaves the work area clean (e.g., rolls up his mat, places the chair under the table, sponges his desk).

4. Setup and cleanup are as much a part of learning as the task itself.

CARE OF EACH OTHER

1. Children are free to work alone or with others, talking softly and enjoying each other's company.

2. Older children often teach and help younger children. Children learn by observing each other and by the act of teaching.

3. Respect for each other is encouraged by the teacher's respect for each child. Courtesy is taught. The children become kind to each other.

A new child entering this environment quickly assimilates the mores of the classroom. Because structure allows freedom, the children are generally happy. Both in normal classes and in learning-disabled classes, serious behavior problems are rare. The children are productive and self-directed—a goal of Montessorians and of all teachers.

14. How to Give a Montessori Lesson

Just as a regular teacher can structure for behavior using the Montessori philosophy, she can also give a Montessori lesson using any type of material. The following are general guidelines.

1. Have the materials in good order and completely prepared before the lesson is started.

2. Give a lesson to a child who is not working rather than to a child who is already absorbed in his work.

3. Prepare the work space: a clear space at a table, an individual mat on the floor, or an empty desk.

4. Invite the child to come to the shelf with you so that he can see the exact location of the materials.

5. Take the child and the material to the work space. Sit beside him on his dominant side.

6. As simply as possible, tell the child the name of the task. If he can assimilate it, tell him the names of the parts of the task.

7. Lay the task out on the table. Use slow, deliberate movements.

8. Demonstrate the task yourself. Use only pertinent language. Make the demonstration interesting. Invite limited participation. If appropriate, show the child how to clean up.

9. Invite the child to do the task. Stay and help him if necessary. Do not give him any more help than he needs.

10. If he wishes to repeat the task, withdraw yourself, but watch

him so that you can help him if he cannot do it on his own.

11. Help the child clean up and replace the material on the shelf if he cannot do it on his own, but do not give any more help than he needs.

12. Do not correct him constantly. If the child makes mistakes, simply present the lesson another day. "Teach teaching, not correcting."

THREE-PERIOD LESSON OF SEGUIN

This is the most essential type of lesson given in the Montessori classroom. It is through this lesson that we teach names of things such as geometrical shapes, and types of dinosaurs; qualities such as blue and green and rough and smooth; sounds of the alphabet with the sandpaper letters; words that follow no rules with the puzzle word slips; geographical labels such as the names of the continents and the countries of Europe. Through this lesson, the child is given the language, the vocabulary, of his culture.

This lesson was not developed by Montessori. She borrowed it from Edouard Seguin, who founded a school for "deficients" in Paris in the mid-1800s. Seguin's successful work with these children influenced Montessori greatly.

It is a simple lesson. It takes less than five minutes and can be given to an individual, a group, or a class. It can be made into a game.

Most important is the use of simple language. The teacher must not use any extra words. She wants to call attention to the vocabulary she is teaching, not to herself. This is especially important for the learning-disabled child, as it is often difficult for these children to determine the important words in a sentence. They have a hard time screening out the essential from the nonessential. If the teacher says, "This is a circle—like wheels, the sun, our round table, and my polka dots," the child will probably forget circle and remember the sun and that it is a nice day to play outside.

Before giving the lesson, the teacher must clear the work space of every unnecessary object. A child will have a difficult time concentrating on the lesson if there are extra crayons, blocks, or puzzle parts at which to look. Often a learning-disabled child has a difficult time determining what is important to see as well. Each thing around him may have equal importance, or he may focus on a bit of dust on the desk rather than on the objects displayed.

So we reduce auditory (language) and visual (objects) distractions in our attempt to structure for successful learning.

Present three objects that contrast greatly. For example, when you are teaching color, begin with red, blue, and yellow rather than pink, red, and orange. When you are teaching geometrical shape, choose a triangle, a circle, and a square to start with rather than a square, a rectangle, and a parallelogram.

It is important, too, that when you are teaching one quality, such as shape, that it not be confused with another quality, such as color. In the Montessori materials, all the color tablets are rectangles and all the shapes in the geometry cabinet are blue. The quality to be learned is isolated. The child is not confused by being shown a red circle, a blue triangle, and a yellow square. One learning-disabled child who learned colors from mixed shapes insisted, when the teacher tried to teach him shape with the same materials, that the red circle was "red" rather than a "circle."

As the name suggests, the lesson has three periods or parts. They are:

1. naming by teacher (information)
2. recognition by student (practice)
3. naming by student (test)

For example, to teach colors, the teacher will select three contrasting colors, clear the work space, and gain the attention of the child.

First Period: naming by teacher. Point as you name. Speak distinctly. "This is red. This is blue. This is yellow."

Second Period: recognition by student, who points when asked by the teacher, "Show me blue. Show me yellow. Show me blue."

This is the most important period of the lesson, since this is when the child learns the names by practice in recognition. Extend this period. Make it interesting and fun, but still use simple language. "Where is yellow? Point to blue. Give me red. Close your eyes. I am going to mix up the colors. OK. Open your eyes. Show me blue. Find red. Give me yellow."

When the teacher is sure the child can recognize the colors and will be successful with the third period, she goes on to that period. If, however, the child cannot recognize the colors, she thanks him, puts the materials away, and repeats the lesson another day. It is important that the child not fail.

Third Period: naming by student. Teacher points to each color and says, "What is this? What is this? What is this?"

The child replies, giving the names of the colors. He is successful. He has learned. The teacher gives quiet approval, and together they replace the materials on the shelf.

To teach the rest of the colors, the teacher will first review the colors learned and then introduce three more colors in the same manner.

This, then, is the lesson used successfully in Montessori classrooms to teach such language as color names, sounds of the alphabet, decimal system terms (1s, 10s, 100s, 1000s), countries of the world, and correct names of leaf shapes (spatulate, orbiculate, hastate). It can be used to teach complex language. With this lesson, children can learn the simple names of the parts of the body and the complex names of the parts of a flower.

The three-period lesson is especially useful in teaching the child with learning disabilities, since it breaks the learning into small steps, reduces distraction, and leads in a structured manner to success.

FIRST AID FOR THE LEARNING-DISABLED CHILD IN THE REGULAR CLASSROOM

What do you do if you are a regular classroom teacher and you suspect that one child in your class has learning problems? You have twenty-five other children and no special training to teach children with learning problems. What can you do? Are any of Montessori's ideas helpful to you?

There are two things you can do. First, continue to observe the child carefully to determine his needs. Second, within your classroom, you can provide structure which will make the rules clear, you can plan individual lessons to the level of the child, and you can be sure the child is successful in his learning.

It is important to recognize, however, that in spite of your best efforts, the child may still require special teaching. The sooner he receives it, the better off he will be. When learning-disabled children develop severe behavior problems, as they quite often do, their learning problems are compounded.

Observation and Referral

The child may be having difficulty learning. No matter how often you explain borrowing in subtraction, he cannot understand it. He seems to know it one day, only to forget it or get it all mixed up the next. He keeps transposing numbers. He writes *18* for *81*. No wonder he can't subtract correctly.

During recess time, you notice he sometimes hits other children and on other days he plays by himself or just watches. He cannot kick the ball well. He misses it frequently. It looks like he is not sure which foot to use.

During story time, he is often fidgety. He cannot sit still. He watches the clock, especially when it makes that loud click periodically, but none of the other children seem to notice it.

Now that you think about it, you recall that he often bumps into walls when trying to go through a door, he's the only child who drops his coat on the floor instead of hanging it on the hook, he spills his milk at least once a week, and he cannot speak a sentence with the words in the correct order. Lately he has become angry without any apparent reason. He is becoming a behavior problem in class.

This awareness of problems requires:

1. that the teacher record her observations to determine the exact nature and frequency of difficulty and to make sure her recollections are accurate and useful

2. that she not allow these problems to go unnoticed or uncared for, as they probably will only get worse in time

3. that she have a conference with the parents to report her objective observations, ask for their observations, and suggest possible referral sources for testing and possibly special tutoring or schooling

Referral sources depend on the resources of the community. Some public schools do excellent testing to determine learning problems and place the children in classes to help them achieve. Others have waiting lists a year long for testing and placement. Often the pediatrician is the person to start with. He can rule out medical, hearing, and vision problems. Many optometrists do testing for visual perception (understanding) as well as visual acuity (ability to see). Some communities have psychologists who privately test intellectual and learning abilities and emotional functioning and give an informative report to the parents with concrete suggestions for help. Some communities have excellent private special-education schools that have a reputation for teaching children in innovative and successful ways.

So you have clinically observed the child, honestly conferred with the parents, and made suggestions to them about where to go for further diagnosis and possible placement. The child is still in your class, however. It is not that you don't like him, it is just that he cannot keep up with the others and he is not behaving well. How do you teach him?

There are three important ideas to remember: structure, individualization, and success.

First Aid Within the Classroom

Structure

1. Provide your special child with positive guidelines for behavior. Make only a few clear rules and enforce them consistently.
2. Plan the daily activities and tell him how his time will be spent. His anxiety will lessen if he knows his general schedule. You may find it useful to write the schedule down for him.
3. Give him a quiet, unstimulating, but not punitive place to work. An office or a study carrel in the back of the class or near your desk may be the best place.

Individualization

1. Since he will probably not be able to keep up with the class in all subject areas, it will be necessary to make some special lessons to give more practice on some skills or facts.
2. Teach him according to his strengths. Verbal explanations are best if he learns through hearing, objects to move and touch if he

learns with his hands, things to look at if he learns best with his vision.

3. Determine where he is successful and start him a bit below that level in order to build up his self-confidence. Help him move forward as rapidly as possible.

4. Give him concrete materials and manipulable equipment, not just paper-and-pencil tasks. If he is frustrated, he will usually calm down when given something to do with his hands.

5. Include him in as many group lessons as he can manage comfortably.

Success

This structure and individualization will help the child achieve success. You can help further:

1. Analyze the tasks you want him to perform and demonstrate each step slowly.

2. Give lessons in segments equal to his attention span—it will lengthen as he feels successful.

3. Praise him sincerely but quietly when he does his work well. Let parents know of his accomplishments through conferences, notes, phone calls.

4. Encourage him to have friends. Give him responsibilities to carry out in the classroom.

Provide opportunities for small successes, which will lend to increased self-esteem and a happier child. You may find that you are able to teach your special child in your regular classroom. You will probably find that all your students, not just your special one, learn more easily with structure, individualization, and success.

15. Montessori, Art, and the Learning-Disabled

by Anne Hyland

Two weeks after I began teaching art to students at Leary School, I concluded that standard methods were not going to give these learning-disabled children the success they needed. Modification of the program so as to keep failure as far away from them as possible seemed the logical solution.

After Marjorie Foster Coburn introduced Montessori to Leary School, I noticed a fascinating similarity between that which I had discovered would work with my art students and the Montessori techniques. Further study of the Montessori system showed me that I could adapt or use directly many of the basic Montessori techniques in teaching art.

The primary tool I had used in the development of a success-oriented program was observation—close, constant, and curious search for the why of the failures in art experienced by so many of the learning-disabled. I found it necessary to examine the details of every movement made by these students, keeping firmly in mind normal motor control and learning sequences from my own experience. This observation and analysis gave me the basis for a method of teaching art to the unsuccessful child. Observation, of course, is also pure Montessori.

As I continued to question and seek answers, I rounded a mental

corner one day and found an idea staring at me: Creativity is generally blocked unless the skills are there to uncork the creative juices.
More simply put: skills first, creativity after. Oh well. Nothing is
new under the sun; before I was born, Maria Montessori stressed
priority for mastery of skills.

My own belief is that not everyone is particularly creative in art.
Perhaps *creative* is not the appropriate word to use for a person's
first experiments with art materials. Rather, he is learning something
new and developing skills. Too many children and adults are pressured into trying to be creative, when what they really need is to be
taught some skills so that they can have fun with art and use it for
self-expression.

The importance of the mastery of skills holds as true for the child
of limited artistic talent as for his more gifted peer. The more creative child uses his skills as tools for further development; the more
limited child uses his skills as a means of making a satisfactory pro-
duction of which he, too, can be proud. A prepared environment
and a structured lesson are conducive to nurturing artistic potential.

Other uses and adaptations of Montessori techniques are as fol-
lows:

1. Create an environment by suggesting that art is fun—serious
fun, important fun—but do not take up the easily penetrated pose of
"Look how creative we're going to be today, kids!" Make the physical environment as attractive as possible, with a minimum of visual
distractions. Use closed cabinets or put window shades over open
shelves.

2. Prepare the lessons in advance. The teacher must practice the
lesson, and it is helpful if she produces an example of what the children are being encouraged to make. Without an example to look at,
the child may well find it hard to visualize the end result. The example gives him something to aim for. In short lessons, it is a good idea
to make the sample with the children watching. Prepare all materials, but do not distribute them immediately if the children are easily
distracted. In such cases, demonstrate part of the lesson first, then
distribute the materials when the children are ready to begin.

3. Structure each lesson for the child's age, abilities, and needs.
Try to arrange matters so the child will be involved in the project
with minimal help, but be prepared to come to his assistance when
necessary with verbal, visual, or manual repetition of the process.

Remember that the lesson is not a problem-solving exercise. It is more important to help the child master a skill than to be a purist about never touching his work. How frustrating it can be for him otherwise!

4. Build the lesson on a step-by-step basis. Poor visual and auditory memory and poor sequencing skills can defeat the success of the project. Too long a sequence can easily frustrate both child and teacher. Program the lesson into small segments whenever necessary and have the child complete one step before you demonstrate the next.

5. Combine teaching methods. To reach a classful of children at different levels of ability, first demonstrate each segment of the lesson visually, without speaking, and then repeat it both visually and verbally.

6. Observe—observe—observe. Try to develop "antennae" and a questioning mind: What is he doing? Why? What can I do to make the lesson easier to comprehend and accomplish? Tailor the lessons to fit the child's abilities.

7. Choose lessons that will meet the child's need to develop basic life skills. Examples of areas to cover: fine motor skills, eye-hand coordination, visual perception, visual discrimination, tactile discrimination, visual and auditory sequencing.

8. Create an atmosphere of confidence for the child by expecting more from him than he thinks he can do, while making sure the lesson is tailored for success—stretch him a little!

Curiosity has led me to try some of these teaching techniques on normal learners. It is highly rewarding. The children get excited, learn quickly, make attractive things, and go away happy. This, too, reminds me of Montessori, whose methods are used successfully with the difficult learners, the average, and the bright.

SECTION FOUR

*How Parents Can Provide the Best Education
for the Learning-Disabled Child*

16. Indications of Present or Potential Learning Disability

As parents, you may notice that your child has some characteristics that disturb you. If your child is already in school, his teacher may notice them as well and may call your attention to them. These characteristics exist in some form or degree in many children at some stage of their development; if your child has some of them, this does not necessarily mean that he is learning-disabled.

Everyone has learning strengths and weaknesses. Some people learn best through seeing, others learn best through hearing. Some learn best by using their hands and through their own experience. A learning weakness is a problem only if it interferes significantly with the potential for learning. In that case, special teaching can strengthen the learning weakness—the disability—and bring the student closer to his potential.

If the learning problem exists for any length of time or if several exist in combination, it would be wise to consult your pediatrician. There may be no reason to be alarmed, but it could be that your child is having learning problems, emotional problems, or is a slow learner. Your pediatrician should be able to refer you for help in your community.

The earlier you catch the learning problem and do something about it, the better chance your child has of avoiding emotional problems resulting from frustration and teasing and rejection from friends. It is generally recognized that the older the child is the more problems he will have and the more difficult working with him will be. Usually his anger and frustration cause behavior problems and, possibly, predelinquent or delinquent behavior. It is best, then, to recognize the problem and seek a solution as soon as possible. Briefly, a child may show the following characteristics:

PRESCHOOL CHILDREN (ages 3–6)

Language

1. does not speak, or does not speak clearly even after age three
2. does not appear to understand directions
3. cannot name objects
4. is not interested in stories

Movement

1. late in sitting, crawling, standing, walking
2. cannot climb stairs easily or ride a tricycle
3. drops things
4. is clumsy and often falls
5. lacks control of body and hands
6. when coloring pictures, is unable to keep the color within the lines

Independent Functioning

1. cannot dress himself in simple clothing
2. cannot eat fairly neatly
3. cannot remember the steps required to wash his hands or put on outside clothing
4. overdependent on his mother

Behavior Problems

1. restless and easily excited
2. cannot adhere to any task for any length of time
3. often has temper tantrums and is easily frustrated

4. is withdrawn or listless

5. at nursery school, is dependent, whiny, belligerent, or unable to fit into the group

Perceptual Problems

1. cannot hear, feel, smell or taste accurately
2. perceives his surroundings as moving rather than stable
3. cannot move in his environment comfortably

Medical Problems

1. excessively susceptible to allergies, ear infections, and upper-respiratory illnesses.
2. when a baby, either unusually lethargic or unusually active

ELEMENTARY AGE CHILDREN (6–12)

Learning: unable to read or to respond to classroom teaching methods.

Reading

1. does not know the sounds of the alphabet
2. cannot blend sounds into words
3. does not remember words learned from one day to the next
4. miscalls words, reverses, guesses

Math

1. does not remember addition combinations, multiplication tables
2. does not understand mathematical concepts

Handwriting

1. cannot form letters
2. cannot copy from the board
3. reverses letters and words

Movement

1. clumsy
2. poor at outside games
3. cannot catch a ball

Behavior

1. unable to concentrate, short attention span
2. distractible
3. disturbs others

Emotions

1. unhappy
2. feels less worthy than his brothers and sisters
3. fearful
4. withdrawn or aggressive
5. easily angered or frustrated
6. does not have many friends of his own age

ADOLESCENTS (13–18)

Academic

1. Increasingly behind in school work
2. has difficulty with conceptual or writing tasks

Social

1. few, if any, friends
2. truancy
3. law-breaking

Emotional

1. lack of self-esteem
2. easily frustrated

3. aggressive or withdrawn
4. unhappy

None of the above taken alone means your child has a learning problem. However, if many of these conditions exist over a period of time, you should do some further investigating. Seek the resources in your community for testing to determine if there is a significant problem. Your pediatrician or school should be able to refer you to a psychologist, an academic diagnostician, or a learning-disabilities clinic. Some public schools do testing, but they often have long waiting lists, so parents sometimes find it worthwhile to seek private testing. Your diagnostician should give you a complete report of the results and interpret them for you. Ask questions to make sure you understand the findings. If the results show that your child is in need of special teaching, the tester will recommend this to you and should be able to refer you to several sources of help in your community.

It is important that you observe your child, have him tested if you suspect learning problems, and if they exist, make sure he gets treatment. Your child deserves the best you can give him.

17. How to Choose a Special School

If your child needs a special school or class, you must be careful to choose a good one. Your child does not have time to waste.

1. Seek a referral to several schools through your doctor, psychologist, principal of your local public school, parents of other students.

2. Make an appointment to visit each school and, if possible, observe the class in which the school principal says your child would be placed.

Watch for happy, productive children; a class of twelve students or less; an orderly, clean environment with learning materials you yourself would like to explore; a teacher who is confident, calm, and warm, who laughs easily, and with whom you feel comfortable. Check your reaction: Did you feel comfortable there? When you took your child for a visit, did he like it?

Your child will spend a good deal of his time at the school. He should feel pleased that he may be going there (although he will be a bit apprehensive at first and need support from you until he has become used to the new school).

Ask about the following:

1. Admission procedures. Testing should be required so that your

child's needs will be known and planned for instead of the teacher discovering them through trial and error.

2. Teacher qualifications and experience. The teacher should be certified by the state or working toward that certification. If the class is a Montessori class, make sure the teacher has had a full year of Montessori training beyond her bachelor's degree. Needless to say, an experienced teacher is usually better than a new one.

3. Support staff. A good teacher is essential, but she is not the whole story. There should be available—and preferably on the staff—a psychologist, an educational diagnostician, a speech therapist, and a motor development specialist. Ask also about programs and staff for a school library, including interesting books to check out and instruction in library skills. There should also be time devoted to art, music, and physical education. An outdoor program which includes hiking, backpacking, and camping is a useful and enjoyable way of building self-esteem and social skills.

4. Philosophy of the School.

a) What is the school's general purpose? It should be to return the child to a regular school or regular class as soon as possible.

b) Curriculum. It should emphasize the basic skills of reading, writing, and mathematics, and it should parallel the instruction the child would be receiving in a regular class in order to prepare him for eventual return. The program for each child needs to be individualized.

c) Methods of Behavioral Management. The school should emphasize the positive. There should be methods of gently praising the child and ways to communicate to the parents achievements in work and behavior. A structured class with clear rules for behavior and a positive approach will aid in managing even the most unmanageable behavior.

5. Success of Former Students.

a) Where are they now?

b) Did they leave close to or on their grade levels?

c) Do they ever return to the school for a visit?

6. Communication with the Teacher.

a) Number of Conferences. There should be at least one planned conference a quarter between the parents and teachers to discuss progress, problems, and future plans. There also should be provision for conferences to be called by the parent or the teacher if either wishes to discuss a particular problem. Frequent meetings are necessary if both are to work together for the good of the child.

b) Written Reports. These should be written once a quarter and should not be just letter grades or a series of check marks. The teacher must clearly state the learning goals she has for the child and thoroughly describe his progress toward those goals.

c) Telephone Conferences. In order to encourage close communication between parents and teachers, telephone contact is necessary. You should be able to call the teacher during school hours and expect her to return your call when she is finished teaching. Likewise, she should feel free to call you when your child makes outstanding progress or if there is a problem that she needs to discuss.

d) Individual Educational Plan. This plan should set the needs of the child, the goals in his education, and the methods of achieving those goals. These goals should include abilities in academic subjects and social skills. Working together as a team in setting the goals, the student, parents, and teacher are more likely to meet them.

7. Parent Involvement.

a) General Parent Meetings. There should be at least two general meetings of the parents during each school year. Traditionally the first meeting in October is an open house, so that the parents can meet the school staff and visit the classrooms. It is fun to sit in your child's desk and imagine what his day is like. You will understand better what your child is telling you about school.

The second or subsequent meetings vary in subject matter. They may deal with a new program, fund raising for the school, or new legislation affecting your child's education.

b) Other types of meetings. Schools vary in the type of meetings they offer parents, depending on the interest expressed by the parents. In class or age-group meetings, it is understood that parents of preschool children have more in common with parents of other young children than parents of teenagers. Often parents with children in the same age group find it is profitable to meet and discuss concerns peculiar to that age group, such as toilet training or dating. It is good to know that other parents are having trouble with night wetting or curfew and useful to share solutions to the problems of parenting.

In discussion groups, parents of children of different ages meet together to discuss general principles that apply to all ages. There may be a series of meetings led by a counselor, a psychologist, or teachers to discuss a particular parenting skill. One series of meetings may be held on the importance of catching the child doing something good while ignoring as much of the bad behavior as possible. Why and how to implement this principle of positive reinforcement may be the topic for a series of parent meetings. Another series may deal with the idea of natural consequences in an attempt to help the child accept responsibility for his own actions.

c) Classroom Observation. You should feel welcome to visit your child's class. Often schools invite parents to observe a class so that the parent can see his child at work. A short conference following the observation will answer questions and clarify it. Parent observation appears to be the most useful for children under twelve, since they are less self-conscious than older children. Even if his own child is self-conscious, the parent will get an idea of what an hour in the school day is like and see the children at work. It is important that the parent sit quietly and avoid talking to the students so that he does not inadvertently disturb the structure of the class. Young children soon become used to observers and continue their work as if no one were watching them.

d) Parent Input Regarding Educational, Social and Emotional Goals. Parents should feel welcome at the school and should be active in planning for their children. The purpose of the meetings, discussion groups, observations, and conferences is for you to know your child and his needs even better and to enable you to plan for him at home and help plan for him at school. During the conferences with the teacher, you will want to discuss your child's educational, social, and emotional needs, the goals and the methods of meeting those goals or objectives. Parents and teachers should work together as a team for the good of the child, and will be able to do this best by sharing their knowledge.

18. Typical Movement Through Learning-Disability Detection, Diagnosis, and Remediation

Learning-disabled children have different problems at different ages. However, most children move through the same general patterns of discovery and remediation. The older the child is when the problem is diagnosed, the more likely it is that he will have emotional problems (secondary emotional overlay) as well.

This secondary emotional overlay, a result of academic failure, takes the form of frustration and anger or withdrawal from friends and academic challenges. Angry children are more likely to receive help than withdrawn children because they cause more trouble. Behavior problems usually cause intensified negative reactions from friends, teachers, and parents, which in turn result in further loss of self-esteem for the children. The situation may snowball into an emotional problem which appears at first glance to be the main difficulty but, in fact, can be traced to the original learning disability. In order to help a child in this state effectively, both the learning disability and the emotional disturbance must be treated.

It is preferable, therefore, to recognize learning problems before emotional problems occur. The earlier they are recognized and treated, the better chance the child has of feeling good about himself. The treatment will also be less complicated and shorter.

SCREENING/TESTING/DIAGNOSIS

Sometimes it is the teacher who reports academic failure and/or behavior problems to unbelieving, shocked, or angry parents. More often the parents have had difficulty managing the child and are aware that something is amiss. Relatives and friends may have made comments, and the parents may have felt inadequate.

Now the parents are embarked on a course of working through the maze of diagnosis and remediation. Often they will find that the diagnosis they hear depends on the specialty of the person diagnosing. And often the problem is diagnosed but possible solutions are not even mentioned. It is best, therefore, to work with a multidisciplinary team of medical, psychological, and educational specialists.

Pediatrician

Start with your child's doctor. State everything you have noticed clearly so that the doctor will have all the facts. Most pediatricians are now aware of learning disabilities and developmental difficulties and are unlikely simply to say that the child will grow out of it.

Your doctor may find nothing medically wrong or may refer you to a neurologist, a speech pathologist, or an allergist for further examination. In any case, he can refer you to the following specialty areas for aid in the diagnosis of the condition and prescribing the correct treatment:

Eyes, Ears and Speech

Physical disabilities must be diagnosed and corrected. A child may simply have a physical disability of eye or ear, and when that is corrected he will have no trouble with learning. Speech therapy can often improve indistinct speech and trouble with using words.

Psychological Testing

Intelligence testing assesses the child's potential and his learning strengths and weaknesses. A good series of psychological tests will also include measures of perceptual abilities (how well the child understands what he sees and hears), language processing (how the child takes in language, processes information, and communicates to others), and emotional functioning (how the child feels about himself). If the tests suggest that the child has severe emotional problems, a referral will be made to a psychiatrist for further diagnosis or therapy.

As parents, you need a complete oral report and a written one as well. You are the main decision makers for your child and need all the facts in order to make the best plans for him.

Educational Testing

The educational assessment may be done by a psychologist or an academic diagnostician. A good educational assessment will include measures of grade levels in reading and math and will break skills down into component parts. For instance, reading tests will include how well a child reads aloud (oral), how well he reads to himself (silent), how well he understands (comprehension), how he pronounces unknown words by saying the sounds of the letters (sound blending), and how he figures out words (word-attack skills). Tests of a young child will show if he is making the expected progress in walking, talking, and independent functioning.

When the child is already at school, his educational history is taken by the academic diagnostician, and conclusions are drawn about how the child learns best in the classroom. This information is considered when the diagnostician reports on the child's learning needs (diagnosis) and suggested teaching procedures (prescription). Again, the parents should receive a complete verbal and written report and may wish to ask that the diagnostician communicate with the present or future teacher to insure that the recommendations are followed.

PLACEMENT/PROGRAMMING

Once the physical, psychological, and educational facts have been gathered, if physical, intellectual, and/or severe emotional difficulties have been eliminated and learning disabilities have been found, the best thing for the child is an educational program. There are several options, depending on the severity of the child's problem, the resources of the parents, and what educational facilities are available locally.

1. A regular school class with after-school tutoring. Often a child can learn with a bit of extra help in a few basic skills. Work on an individual and regular basis may help him catch up with his classmates. It is important that the tutor and teacher communicate and cooperate in working toward the same goals so that the child is helped rather than confused.

2. A regular school class with in-school "resource room"—help from a special teacher who works with the classroom teacher in strengthening weak areas. The student leaves his classroom for a few hours a week, receives the special help individually or in a small group, and remains in the classroom for his other subject areas.

3. Special classes for weak academic subjects and regular classes for nonacademic subjects such as physical education and art.

4. Special classes for all subjects so that the child is given more chance to succeed and is not presented with too stimulating an environment.

5. A special school with classes of eight to ten students and a total and intensive educational and social environment geared to the needs of the learning-disabled child with the goal of returning him to a regular school as soon as possible.

Leary School is a good example of a special school for learning-disabled children. Its procedures, described below, are typical.

PRELIMINARY CONTACT

The first step is a telephone conversation with the admissions coordinator. She makes a preliminary decision as to whether the school is suitable for the child. If so, parents are given an appointment one or two weeks later for an initial interview with one of the directors. The parents are sent the school's brochures, statement of philosophy, and a form to be filled out with general information about the child, which is returned to the school prior to the interview. The parents arrange to have sent to the school teachers' comments, previous school records, and the records of psychological, psychiatric, or educational tests if any have been done.

The director of the unit dealing with the child's age group studies all this material before the initial conference in order to get a view of what the child needs. Usually both parents and the child visit the school and attend the conference.

Occasionally a parent will come without the child to assess the school before bringing the child into the picture. The parents are welcome to visit the classes into which the child might be placed to observe educational techniques, teacher's style, potential classmates, and the general atmosphere of the class.

INITIAL INTERVIEW

If the child is brought to the initial interview, he is often invited to visit the class in which he is most likely to be placed. This gives him a chance to explore the classroom and gives the teacher an opportunity to observe him and diagnose his needs informally. Usually the children like the secure, protected environment and say so happily after the visit.

The purpose of the initial interview is to gather information about the child's problems and give information about the school's program. It usually lasts about one hour.

The director asks about the child's problems, why the parents are thinking of changing schools, what the teachers say about him, how he gets along at home and in the neighborhood, what he enjoys doing, what his strengths are, how the parents discipline him, what they feel his educational needs are.

The parents usually ask about the school day, the size of the class, the methods of teaching, the qualifications of the staff, and the availability of speech therapy, play therapy, physical education, art, music, and library programs. They see the classrooms and the resource areas for individual or small-group work with a teacher's aide and so can tell if their child would be happy there.

The child is usually asked a few questions about himself. "How do you like school? What is your favorite activity after school? What is your favorite TV program?" He is also given an opportunity to ask questions: "Do you have physical education? Will I have homework? Why do these kids come here?"

Testing is discussed. If the child needs testing, arrangements are made to have it done. The purpose of the testing is to provide the most data possible about the child's strengths and weaknesses so that an educational program can be planned in the most efficient manner. The child will not be subject to trial-and-error teaching and he will not waste time.

Some preschool children are too immature for psychological and educational testing. Since giving them a fair score on a test is nearly impossible, the formal testing requirement is often waived. In this case, classroom observation and informal diagnosis is the best for the child. By the conclusion of the initial interview, the parents and the director have a pretty good idea of whether the school is right for the child.

FINAL INTERVIEW

The purpose of the final conference is for the parents and the director to decide jointly, on the basis of the testing and interviewing, if the school can help the child.

If the testing or evaluation has been done at the school by the staff psychologist, she too attends the final conference to discuss her findings with the parents and give them a copy of her written report. The parents can read it again later and ask further questions.

They discuss whether the child will start at the school. The staff psychologist observes the classes, consults with the teachers, and does therapy with some of the students; she is thoroughly familiar with the program and can tell if school and child will suit each other. The director, of course, knows how many places are available and whether it is advisable to accept the child. The facts are openly discussed with the parents and the decision is made together.

If it is decided that the child should not attend the school because his problems are either too severe or not severe enough to benefit from the program, other possible programs in the community are discussed. The director can refer the parents to other places where they may find more suitable help. The testing and diagnosis has clarified the problem and aids in getting the help most useful to the child.

If it is decided that the child should attend the school, plans for him are discussed, including class placement and the possible need for speech or psychological therapy. The parents are encouraged to relax a bit and allow the new school time to help. The team relationship begins with the parents and school working for the child's benefit.

Now the child has gone through a series of steps: problem recognition, screening for physical problems, educational and psychological testing, and admission to a new school. The next step is to meet his new teacher, if he has not already done so.

MEETING THE TEACHER

If the child enters at the beginning of the school year, he meets his teacher during a preschool visit, if he enters in the middle of the year, he meets her during a visit to her class. The teacher talks with the child, shows him around the classroom, and makes him feel comfortable. At the same time, she is observing his interests and behavior closely and clinically. She is looking for the clues that will show her how to help him progress. She may show him how to do something in which he shows an interest and will do well. Usually the child asks a few questions about the daily schedule, the location of his desk, and the rules of the class. He is discovering the structure, the ground rules for his behavior. This gives him some security and comfort for the scary adventure of starting at a new school.

PLANNING/PRESCRIBING

After all the information has been gathered and interpreted and the child's needs are known, the director composes "The Individual Education Plan," which is in effect a general contract between the parents and the school. The plan has two parts. The first part outlines the problem areas as revealed by testing and the child's history (the probable diagnosis). The second part describes the action to be taken (the prescription). For instance, if the child has a speech problem, the plan will call for screening by the speech pathologist with a view to in-school speech therapy. If the child has emotional problems, the plan will call for observation by the staff psychologist with a view to group or play therapy. If there is a need for intensive outside therapy, that is agreed to in the plan. The plan, then, is tailored to the needs of the individual child.

TEACHING/LEARNING

Now the teacher takes over. She spends a considerable amount of time with the child, and her observations are often more valuable than anyone else's. She reviews the file, writes up a résumé of test results, strengths, and weaknesses, and makes a general plan for accurate teaching. After about a month, she writes down a series of behavioral and social/emotional objectives, which are goals for the child and give structure to her teaching.

The children in the Montessori Primary Unit work with both Montessori materials and traditional workbooks and texts. Children of six, seven, and eight who have few or no academic skills start with Montessori materials for learning basic reading and math, and then are introduced to the texts in use in public school when they can manage them. Children who have some academic skills often use textbooks and Montessori equipment simultaneously, the latter giving them concrete experience of the abstractions in the textbook.

GRADUATION

A child is ready to return to a regular school when he is functioning on or close to grade level, when he is capable of dealing successfully with his peers, and when he likes himself. Before the child graduates from the school, his parents are advised about how to continue his development. The teacher helps the parents select the new school and sometimes visits the school to talk with the teachers there. Records and transcripts are sent to the new school.

The school holds a graduation ceremony, complete with certificates, speeches, and refreshments. It is a happy and touching occasion. The students have worked hard to achieve their potential.

19. What Can I Do at Home?

Now that you have recognized that a problem exists and have found a good school or program for your child—what can you do at home?

RELAX . . . for at least a few weeks. You have been through a lot. So has your child. Hug him. Love him. Enjoy him.

You will still need to monitor your child's progress at school, but try not to do it by questioning him. If you have not heard from the teacher after three weeks have passed, call her and ask her how your child is doing.

Although it is difficult, continue to avoid questioning your child about his academic progress. This is important for three reasons:

1. He has had extreme difficulty at school in the past, and he feels he has failed. If you continually question him, you reinforce that feeling of failure.

2. Eventually he will tell you about his budding successes. For the first time, he may enjoy going to school. Praise him gently, expressing confidence in his ability even though he faces a hard task. Be pleased when he gets a good report from school.

3. He needs to feel like an ordinary child, not a problem child or a

learning-disabled child. Concentrate on building his whole person at home.

"Okay," you may say, "I have relaxed, but I still feel I could do more at home. What can I do?"

You can do a lot. As parents, you are the most influential people in your child's life. Your most important task is to give him a feeling of worth and the ability to cope. You can help him by structuring his environment and behavior for success just as the school does.

The following are guidelines based on Montessori theory for you to use in the home. These are merely guidelines. You may choose to use one, many, or none of them. As the child's parent, you know best. Trust yourself. Do what feels comfortable, and it will probably be right for your child as well.

Remember, your child has three main developmental needs:
1. movement
2. language
3. independent functioning

You can plan his environment—physical surroundings, activities available, and adult direction—to meet the individual needs of your child.

Planning the Home Environment

Child's Room

For the young child and for the learning-disabled child, a calm, orderly, manageable personal environment is imperative. The learning-disabled child often overreacts to too much stimulation to eye and ear. If possible, he should have his own room. It may be that his behavior is reflecting disorganization in his environment. Therefore, we suggest:

1. Paint the room a pastel color.

2. Reduce the number of wall decorations—one or two pictures are enough.

3. Provide a bed that is simple to make and show him how to make it in a step-by-step demonstration.

4. Provide a low rod in the closet so he can hang up his own clothing.

5. Provide low shelves for his toys, books, and so on. Each item should have its own place. Difficult as it is, reduce the number of his possessions.

6. Give him a comfortable chair, such as a bean-bag chair or a rocker.

7. A desk cleared of extraneous objects and facing a wall helps him do his homework.

8. A record player may be a nice addition. Listening to stories and music gives him practice in listening for meaning and will help relax him.

The Home in General:

1. Keep the home quiet and peaceful. Try to maintain a calm atmosphere.

2. Have books and magazines available. Read to your child. Discuss pictures.

3. Involve him in the work of the home. Show him how to do simple but necessary chores such as setting the table and caring for plants and pets.

4. Teach him good manners and proper eating habits by your own example.

SUGGESTED ACTIVITIES

Movement

1. Reduce the time during which he watches television. This may be difficult and may have to be done gradually, but it is very important. Watching television is a passive and isolated activity. Your child needs to move around and be with people.

However, it is useful to watch the news together and then discuss current events, places, people. Learning-impaired children often lack a fund of general information. Sharing sports and following teams is often a social activity and involves the child in the fun of the family and the larger world. Some educational programs are beneficial. Watch for special programs and make plans to view them with your child.

However, a child who spends every afternoon watching reruns and violent cartoons is isolating himself and missing the opportunity to play outside, shoot baskets, or ride his bike.

2. Encourage outside play. Good activities, depending on the age and ability of your child, include:

sandbox play

climbing on a gym set

riding wheel toys—tricycles, bicycles, skateboards

shooting baskets

tether ball

Ping-Pong

swimming

You may have to show him how to do these things. Spend time showing him how to throw, kick, and catch a ball. Start with a large ball to make it easy for him and reduce the size of the ball as his ability grows.

3. When your child is ready, encourage him to play a team sport. Many communities, for example, now have soccer programs, which allow each child to have fun without having to be a great player. Many learning-disabled children are excellent soccer players and they are very proud to wear their team shirts to school.

Language

1. Speak clearly to your child. You are his prime language model.

2. If your child has trouble processing or understanding what you say, he may appear to be disobeying or behaving badly when his real difficulty is that he simply cannot remember. To help him:

a) Give a one-step direction ("Please bring in the newspaper").

b) Ask him to repeat the direction.

c) Give him time to carry out the direction.

d) Thank him, referring to the direction: "Thank you for bringing in the newspaper."

e) When he is able to follow one-step directions, give two- or three-step directions.

3. Give your child a good vocabulary. Instead of calling all birds

just *bird,* point out bluejays, robins, woodpeckers. Show him the difference between a holly and an oak tree.

    4. Play games in the car:

    a) Develop the distinction between right and left, asking, "Which way did we turn?"

    b) Point out one or two signs and read them.

    c) Take him with you to do a few errands, and afterward ask him where you both went, in order to build up his ability to think in sequence.

    d) On a familiar short trip, ask him which way you should turn.

    5. Read stories:

    a) Read the same book over and over if your child asks for it. It may be a chore for you, but he needs and wants repetition. After he knows the story, start to leave out key words; he may be able to supply them. If he is just starting to read, read some phonetic books on his reading level. Encourage him to read aloud along with you if he wishes.

    b) Include rhymes and poems when you read aloud. Rhyming is a good aid to learning.

    c) Read some stories that are good children's literature or that you particularly enjoy.

    d) Take him to the public library. Allow him to check out two or three books. Many libraries encourage children to obtain their own cards when they can write their names. Usually children feel very proud and official when they get their own library cards.

    e) Give simple instruction in days of the week, seasons, telling time, address, phone number, parts of the body.

    6. Music:

    a) Listen to music with your child. Point out passages you like or the sounds of particular instruments.

    b) Sing songs.

    c) Encourage him to play an instrument if he shows talent.

Independent Functioning

    1. Self-care. Teach your child how to wash his hands, comb his hair, hang up his clothes, and so on. Demonstrate the actions step by step and then give him time to do it. Give him only the help he

needs. For instance, hand-washing can be broken down into these steps or tasks:

a) Turn on water
b) Wet hands
c) Soap hands
d) Replace soap
e) Rinse hands
f) Turn off water
g) Pick up towel
h) Dry hands on towel
i) Hang up towel

Once you think about the steps involved in the simplest of tasks, you will realize that just saying, "Go wash your hands," may not be enough until you have shown your child how.

Give the small child manageable clothing. Boots should be big enough to go over his shoes. Coats should have large, easy-to-zip zippers. Slacks should have elastic waistbands.

2. Care of the Environment. Encourage your child to take part in the work of the home. Many activities in the home build learning abilities. For example:

a) Setting the table helps with numbers, discrimination between left and right, spatial relationships, ordered sequence.

b) Matching and folding socks helps him discriminate between different things, different colors, and different sizes, and gives him practice in small, precise movements of the hands.

c) Wiping up food he has spilled builds responsibility and understanding of cause and effect, and helps him accept his own mistakes.

d) Cooking and baking helps with numbers, ordered sequence, following directions. Making something makes children feel successful.

When the child does real, needed work in the home, his place in the family is strengthened.

3. Social Relationships. Teach your child how to greet people, answer the phone, introduce himself, excuse himself, and so on. As he learns these skills, he will feel more comfortable in social situations.

Invite his friends home. Sometimes it is best to invite just one friend at a time until he feels comfortable with more.

Encourage him to join a scouting group, take lessons in an area in which he is talented, attend Sunday school, join a team. It is important that he feel himself part of the community.

These are just a few suggestions for activities in the home. You might want to start a parent discussion group to discover and share common experiences with other parents.

Your most important task is to build your child's self-esteem. General guidelines are:

1. React positively to positive behavior. "Catch your child being good." Comment when you are pleased with him and downplay your reaction to poor behavior.

2. Give your child only limited choices. "Would you like oatmeal or Cheerios for breakfast?" "Do you want to wear your blue shirt or your yellow shirt tomorrow?"

3. Structure time as well as space. "After we go to the movie, we will have ice cream." "It is four o'clock now. In two hours, we will leave." "You may finish that game and then it is time for bed."

4. Prepare your child for new experiences. "At the concert, we will relax and listen to the music. During the intermission, we will get up and take a walk."

5. Take time for yourself. Hire a sitter and go out. You need time to be yourself and will be a better parent after a little time and distance away from your child.

Questions most often asked by parents are:

What toys should I buy?

Limit your child's possessions. Too many things are not only unnecessary but also confusing; they hinder rather than help. Good toys, depending on your child's age and development level, are:

Age 2–7: wooden puzzles, blocks, Tinkertoy sets, clay, records, stuffed animals, trucks, dolls, tricycles, balls, books

Age 6–10: jigsaw puzzles, cards, games, erector sets, Lego blocks, bikes, jumpropes, sports equipment, musical instruments, books, art supplies

Age 10–15: craft kits, sports equipment, more sophisticated games, records, art supplies

What do I do about poor behavior?
1. Give the child a quiet place to go to calm down—a "time out" or "quiet spot."
2. Then discuss what upset him.
3. Suggest alternative ways of solving the problem the next time.

What about diet?
Nutrition is very important. Avoid food that contains refined sugar; give the child a diet rich in protein. Give him cheese and peanuts for snacks rather than cookies. Some research into food suggests that artificial colorings and flavorings increase hyperactivity. Many parents have eliminated or reduced sugar and artificial ingredients and have found that their children have become calmer and easier to manage.

Allergies are also common in the learning-disabled child. For a child with allergies, the diet at home and at school must be modified accordingly.

What about medication?
Medication prescribed to reduce hyperactivity is often useful, as it allows the child to calm down. Once he is not directing most of his energy to the task of sitting, he can direct his attention to learning. When he feels solidly successful, his medication can be reduced or eliminated.

What do I tell the grandparents and neighbors? They don't understand.
Explain that your child has trouble with learning, which has made him feel unhappy with himself. You are lucky you have discovered this and you are helping him. When he is taught by special techniques, he will learn. Now you are just enjoying him as a person and helping him feel better about himself. You hope they will help, too.

What will happen to my child when he grows up? Will he ever outgrow this?
A number of very successful and well-known people have had learning disabilities. Trouble with learning is just that, and it can be overcome. Once they have been taught correctly, most children go on to realize their intellectual potential and become valuable members of society.

20. Roger and Sam—Two Who Needed Help

This section consists of two-part case histories of two children, Roger and Sam. The first part is by the child's mother, the second by Marjorie Foster Coburn.

We are grateful to the mothers for sharing their feelings of despair and hope. Perhaps their stories will help other parents of children with learning problems.

ROGER

Where do you begin with the entanglement of an exceptional child? Different? Yes—but only to a degree. For you notice that he is overactive, aware, questioning, talking, and yet emotionally insecure. Discipline, yes, but cautiously, for this child requires and demands unconditional love. Because you love him, you seek out the best possible help for him and are constantly aware of his peers and of the school system that he is to attend. Do they meet *his* needs? No. You must act, but how, where, when? You are in a dilemma!

This was our plight, and because my husband and I wanted Roger to be happy, the searching began. First I requested that a psychological exam be given to him. This only fortified our feelings. His attention span was short for his age: he tended to get stuck doing one thing and was unable to move on to the next task when asked; his abstract reasoning ability was extremely high, but the written word was some villain lurking in the dark. It was all there: the roller coaster behavior of the learning-disabled child. *And* school continued.

Kindergarten—his great personality got him through that one! First grade came; "True desks," as Roger said, "and now I can learn to read." All seemed well for a few months, but then, as more and more demands to conform to the norm were required, Roger became emotionally upset. His teacher worked with him, but Roger's demands were greater than time allowed. He was assigned to be helped by children in upper grades, who found him fascinating! Roger talked his way through all things. What a brilliant child; what a vocabulary!

On to second grade—the frustration continued to mount as his needs were not met, and his peers began to single him out as being different. A reading teacher, through rote drill, and many unhappy experiences for Roger, got him to spell his name.

At this point, I began to seek outside professional help, as we seemed to be getting nowhere with Roger. First, we sought a special reading teacher, outside the school system. This proved beneficial, but at times she became uneasy, as she seemed to feel he really was not trying. A battery of tests was given by a clinical psychologist. We found that Roger was average to above average in intelligence but needed a structured environment. A neurologist was unable to pinpoint any neurological problems, but something was not as it should be. However, the feeling was that Roger could and should do better.

At this point, we decided upon a regular private school for Roger, one where he could have more individual attention, and with a teacher-pupil ratio of one to twelve. Great! He will make it, we just knew. After an interview, a decision to have him repeat the second grade was made. Our hopes were that he would be able to master the academic assignments and thereby strengthen his own self-image.

Friends were sought to reinforce Roger, work with him, and help him over the emotional pitfalls of failure.

A psychiatrist worked with us, pointing to problems, and the dire need of a structured environment. We felt that we were on our way.

The private school was a blessing in disguise. We had hoped that Roger could make it, but stark reality hit us all. Roger could not cope; he fell further behind. Then we knew he simply had to be in a school that knew about and worked effectively with learning-disabled children. He could not remain in that private school.

Being in the field of education, I had developed a keen interest in learning-disabled or dyslexic children, or whatever other name was in vogue at the time. I enrolled in several graduate courses pertaining to the learning-disabled child. I visited various schools specializing in learning disabilities and sought out the county's program in this field. At this time, I enrolled in a county-sponsored class on training as a teacher's aide for the learning-disabled child. I talked with many educators in the field, and began better to understand the fine line between the normal and the exceptional child. It was at this time that my husband and I realized that Roger needed special training, direction and a staff who knew when to let the child seek his creativity and when to hold him to the structured behavior which will enable him to achieve the goals he sets for himself.

Roger was accepted at Leary School, to begin after the fall break.

After three long years of trial and error, reading, talking, hoping, and praying, a great feeling of relief came over me. This was 1973, and he was to enter the Montessori Unit. I knew that we could give the necessary reinforcement at home, following the directions of the school. He was then a child who had been badgered to the degree that he believed that no one liked him. He could not relate to his peers and was angry not only with himself, but with the world in general. Roger's self-esteem had reached its lowest ebb.

It was here, at long last, that trained personnel were ready to recognize and praise his positive traits and habits and to work with him in a planned way so that his faults could be modified one at a time. Roger was able to explore and satisfy his ever-inquiring mind through the Montessori equipment.

We met each day as it came, knowing well that there would be many high and low days. At first there were more low than high ones. Through the patience and understanding of the faculty, Roger became a better friend to himself and to others. He began to attack daily problems with more confidence; he now had a sense of belonging and the thrill of achieving; and he began to be accepted by his peers as the wonderful, inquisitive person that he is.

We still have many hills and dales to travel, but we are well on the way. He has gained confidence in reading and the phonetic approach to the attack of words, and is making more progress in all phases of academic work. His emotional climate has improved a hundredfold.

The proper approach with Roger is most important. We realize that his personality cannot be changed. We must meet him halfway by not putting him in an environment or a social situation which is too difficult for him to handle. He needs a structured household, with a fairly definite daily routine. This also includes various chores which he can handle. We try to aid Roger by making him aware of his own limitations and strengths and how to make the best use of them. I try such techniques as breaking up his work periods and encouraging him to play with just a few friends at a time. It is through this guidance and structure that he is able to have more and better control over his own behavior.

Now that he is nearly eleven and close to the age of puberty, I realize how important it has been to have an early start with the child confronted with learning disabilities. Roger's directions are set, and through guidance and counseling, he knows himself better. How much better that this took place at a younger age. We have the highest hopes for a good and constructive life for Roger in the years to follow.

Roger's parents came to Leary School two and a half years ago to inquire about admission. Roger had been out of school for a month. He was a large, mannerly, anxious-to-please eight-year-old boy. He seemed to want desperately to be liked.

Previous school experiences had been disastrous. He had entered school with high hopes but had not been able to learn to read. After-school tutoring had helped, but there was little carry-over in school. Other children began to regard him as different, and his relationships with them suffered. There were no children of his own age in the neighborhood. He learned to get on better with adults, but he had not learned to play with other children.

His parents were alert to the problems and began to seek solutions. Psychological testing when he was six years old revealed a hyperactive little boy who had difficulty behaving. His ability to express his thoughts was good, but he could not deal with social situations. Testing by a learning-disability specialist indicated that Roger had trouble remembering what he saw and trouble thinking clearly. A structured school environment was recommended.

After not doing well in public school, Roger was placed in a structured private school by his parents, who hoped that there he would make progress. In a few months, it became apparent that he needed not only structure but also special teaching methods. It was then that the parents came to Leary School.

Our psychoeducational testing revealed that Roger was bright and good at remembering facts and using his hands. However, there were markedly lower scores on some parts of the test, which suggested that he did not understand how his actions caused reactions in other people and that he could not accept responsibility for his actions. Although he saw details in pictures and in his environment quite well, he had difficulty seeing the difference between the letters *b* and *d*. He could not distinguish important visual stimuli from unimportant visual stimuli. He was reading on the primer level and could do simple addition and subtraction.

He was friendly and bright, but his learning disabilities and resultant emotional problems were interfering with his ability to learn. He was hyperactive, which made it hard for him to pay attention. He needed external controls and step-by-step instructions to reduce his impulsiveness and help him concentrate. The Montessori environment was recommended.

Roger was placed in the Montessori class of children aged six through nine. He liked the Montessori equipment and was able to talk about what he discovered in his work. He was given individual lessons in learning the sounds of the alphabet and blending them into words. On the playground, he refused to join any organized game, preferring to watch. He loved to draw, and could draw elaborate and detailed pictures. This skill soon drew admiration from his classmates. His greatest love was the library. He would often sit with an encyclopedia and try to read. He could not read it but could follow the ideas through the diagrams and pictures.

Pressure was reduced. We tried to help Roger like himself as a person. When he had difficulty, play therapy was recommended and was initiated by his parents.

During that first year, Roger relaxed and started to learn. The Montessori equipment helped him see correctly and understand what he saw. Drills helped him learn the sounds of the alphabet. The mathematics equipment enabled him to see why the numbers fit together the way they do. The structure of the classroom made him feel secure and protected. The frightened little boy began to learn.

In the following year, he was placed in a less structured all-boy class. He was able to work with workbooks and texts. With praise and guidance, he learned good social behavior and began to enjoy being a boy in the company of other boys. He even started to play soccer with the others in physical education. At the end of this academic year, he was reading and doing math on the second-grade level. In science and social studies, taught with discussion—Roger's strength—he was on the fourth-grade level. During this year, Roger went on an overnight camping and caving trip with his class. He now found it easier to make friends.

Roger is no longer in therapy. He continues to need the supportive structure of the class and the individual teaching. He is now invited to friends' homes after school and is often the one to welcome new students into the building. His ability to think and communicate still allows him to relate well to adults, and he usually asks perceptive questions.

We expect that Roger will return to public school before long. He can now read almost on grade level, and he enjoys math. He has friends and appears to like himself as well. When he is finished with his assignments, Roger loves going to the library. He still reads the encyclopedia, but now he is not pretending.

SAM

In October 1972, after seven years of marriage and no children, the Social Services Department in Fairfax County called to let us know they had a child for us. The social worker described him as a small, fair-haired, blue-eyed two-year-old. She explained he had had spinal meningitis at seven months, but seemed to have suffered no permanent damage. She also added that he "is very, very active."

One week later we met the child at a local shopping center and were completely captivated by his bubbly enthusiasm for exploring. We took to him and he seemed to take to us right away; arrangements were made to sign placement papers the next morning so we could take him home.

The next day was the most exciting day of my life! We took him home and spent the rest of the morning sitting on the floor playing with him. That first day I noticed he moved sometimes just because he could not be still. His speech was a few months behind developmentally, but he could stack blocks very high before they fell.

The first night I noticed he rocked in his bed for at least one hour before going to sleep.

As time went by, I noticed he had great difficulty learning about danger. He just could not stop himself from teasing our dogs. He would run into them, grab their tails, and try to hug them, even though he knew he was not allowed to touch them when he was not on my lap. He became hysterical and at times would throw himself to the floor kicking, screaming, and rolling around.

I decided to discuss this behavior with the doctor, and his response was, "Well, Mrs. Smith, you'll never have a boring moment."

We enrolled him in a local Montessori school (twenty-five children per class) at two and a half years old, and that was a disaster. He would throw equipment around the room and play in the sink. Many times he came home drenched. The teacher was of little help since she was a very young, inexperienced woman and couldn't really handle the normal children. She did tell me, when I picked him up one day, that he seemed to be hyperactive, so again I went to the pediatrician asking for help. No response again.

At this point, I began to read up on hyperkinesis. I decided that Sam certainly fit the profile, so I made arrangements to take him to Boston Children's Hospital for a complete examination. The doctor diagnosed him as hyperkinetic and put him on Dexadrine. Finally we began to make some progress. The administrator at the school Sam was attending recommended that we look into sending him to Leary School.

He started at the school in February 1974. Progress has been slow, as it always is with these children, but improvement has been constant.

Before entering the school, he was evaluated by a psychologist, who found he had an auditory scramble and seemed to perseverate. The auditory problem is probably the most frustrating problem of all with this child.

He was put on Ritalin after one year, since he had begun to experience less effect from the Dexadrine. The Ritalin has continued to be effective.

I remember that I was almost relieved when the doctor at Boston Children's Hospital told me Sam definitely was hyperactive. I guess I had been afraid that maybe there was something wrong with me as a parent. I looked forward to receiving help and was anxious to be able to enjoy raising my son instead of always having conflict. I do thank God for Sam's cheerful nature. His explosions usually take the form of overexcitement instead of aggressive actions.

Over the years, I found a number of avenues for lowering the number and severity of his outbursts. First, the medication has been vital; I still wish he didn't have to take it, but it works. Second, I found there was much benefit from correcting his diet. Foods having little or no nutritive value such as sugar, artificial flavor and color, and highly processed foods have been removed from his diet as much as possible. I always use whole grains, to be certain he gets fiber, and lots of fresh raw vegetables (all kinds). Just because he doesn't drink soda pop or eat candy and potato chips does not mean he doesn't get treats. He loves yogurt, eats ice cream (natural), nuts, seeds, raisins, honey drops, and the like.

Sam loves going to school and is truly learning at an almost normal rate. The staff is trained well and observes problems at their inception. I was so fortunate that he was going to this school during my recent divorce. The school provided him with a stability that might well have been lacking in another type of school. When he began showing some adjustment difficulties, the administrator, teacher, and psychologist evaluated the situation and immediately began play therapy. He responded well and now seems to be on his way to acceptance, if not understanding. The staff was extremely supportive of me during the divorce, and I think such a school more closely approximates school as it should be. The close cooperation between administration, teacher, parent, and child has been a wonderful experience, and I expect continued success.

In conclusion, I would like to express some feelings I have about dealing with the learning-disabled child. Their bodies are working at a disadvantage, and proper nutrition is imperative for growth and development, both physical and emotional. In the area of control, I have found it important to set firm guidelines and to be consistent. Also, when the child begins to lose control, provide a chair he/she may use for "time out." This is a place where he can kick, scream, cry, and so on, but he is not allowed to get off of the chair. Soon he will take himself to the chair for time out when he feels a need.

Most important of all is love. Love them and let them always feel secure in that love. Help them understand that every person has his own problems. Please don't be embarrassed because you have a learning-disabled child. That attitude will increase the difficulties of raising the child. Soon he will be ashamed of himself and then will have a self-image that won't allow for the development of the magnificent person inside. Self-love is where we must all begin. We must accept ourselves, as they must accept themselves, just as we are, because we can only grow from the seed that is within us. We must accept life and love living. The very best advice I can give is to love these children and deal with their problems out of love.

He was an adorable three-year-old boy. Blond, curly hair, a tentative smile, and an inquisitive manner. Sam's parents brought him to the school at the suggestion of the Montessori school he had been attending. Sam had found the school too stimulating. Often he could not follow directions and sometimes was so hyperactive that he had to be carried about in his teacher's arms.

Sam had been adopted at the age of two. His parents reported that he had a tendency to become overexcited, that he had a short attention span and occasional temper tantrums.

Diagnostic and psychological tests indicated that Sam was a hyperactive child who was behind other children his age in understanding the meaning of words and expressing his own thoughts. He could not understand what he heard around him. He mixed up instructions. His ability to understand what he saw was good and his intelligence was above average. It appeared that Sam would learn best through demonstration rather than spoken instructions. He needed more structure and less noise and talking around him. Medication was prescribed to reduce his hyperactivity.

Sam was enrolled in a half-day Montessori class two and a half years ago. There were only seven students, with a teacher and an aide—few children and few materials. In spite of the little work he had been able to accomplish in his regular Montessori school, Sam had absorbed the idea there of choosing work, doing the task, and then returning it to the shelf, and was able to use a few of the materials. When given simple one-step directions in an environment relatively free of noise, he was able to follow instructions. Structure was imperative for him; without it, he became lost and frightened. He needed to know what was expected of him. He had no temper tantrums at school, although he was still hyperactive.

With individual attention and gentle praise, Sam began to work his way through the materials. It soon became evident that he loved to learn. He was happy with himself each time he mastered a new task. Although he was the youngest in the class, he allowed none of the older children to baby him. He regarded them as equals and liked to play with them.

During the next school year, Sam was still taught on a one-to-one basis because of his short attention span. When he progressed to making words with the movable alphabet, the teacher saw that he had trouble using his eyes and hands together. Sandpaper letters were used to help him feel the direction in which the letters go.

Montessori materials were used to help him remember the order of the steps in a task. His body-coordination skills and knowledge of where his body was in space were strengthened by walking along the narrow balance beam and climbing and trampoline activities. Understanding and communication were improved by listening games, which required him to listen, understand, and talk. Sam continued to be curious; he wanted to learn and did. In spite of his hyperactivity and learning disabilities, he seemed to have suffered no loss of self-esteem. Sam liked himself and others.

At the age of five, Sam was the kingpin of his half-day class. He was the most advanced child socially and academically. When his parents separated, the psychologist gave him play therapy, and when he regained security at home, he became his confident self again.

He was starting to read—right on schedule for a child in a Montessori class. However, he often read words from right to left, so he was given intensive work on moving his eyes in a left-to-right direction. Poor use of the hand in small activities became evident. While exercises were increased to strengthen this skill, Montessori tasks not requiring pencil and paper were given to allow him to proceed in math.

At the age of five and a half, Sam was promoted to a full-day Montessori class. He got his first lunch box and was thrilled. Although he was the youngest, he fit into the social group of the eight children aged six through nine. He can now read three- and four-letter phonetic words and can copy on paper the words he spells with the movable alphabet. He knows his numbers one through ten. He continues to get on well with others and can handle his emotions in a normal, healthy fashion.

Sam will return to the school next year, as he continues to need the structure, observation, and intervention of the teachers and the Montessori equipment. With this careful monitoring and meeting of his needs, he is proceeding on schedule academically.

In spite of his hyperactivity and learning disabilities, Sam is learning and continues to be a happy, well-liked, productive little boy. It is fortunate that his parents recognized his problems early, faced them, and provided the help he needed before they were compounded. Without the special help he needed, Sam would not be the self-confident little boy he is today.

21. Montessori and the Learning-Disabled Child: A Summary

Education, according to Maria Montessori, must begin much earlier than has been traditional if the child's full potential for positive development during his formative period is to be realized. This is especially true of the learning-disabled child, who should be identified early and provided the comprehensive educational services necessary to meet his individual needs.

The educational implications for learning-disabled children during the various *sensitive periods*, as Maria Montessori termed them, should be further explored and provision made to utilize each period in the educational process. Likewise, the implications of Montessori's other concepts for the learning-disabled child, such as the *absorbent mind*, need additional study and application. Perhaps if children with a predisposition toward minor learning disabilities received the opportunities provided in a Montessori classroom during the period of the absorbent mind (ages 3–6), some of the learning weaknesses could be strengthened or avoided.

Education for the learning-disabled child, as for all children, should consist of help toward positive development rather than expensive, fragmentary, and often ineffective efforts at remediation. Reduction of defects through proper education must be given priority. Ideally, education is an intrinsic process of doing by the child, of

177

his "becoming," in the sense of self-development. Traditionally, education has been largely an external process of "doing to" or at best "doing for" the child, but the educator should help the child do it himself.

The Montessori prepared environment offers the learning-disabled child a world in which he can teach himself, free from the demands and distractions of the adult-centered environment. Here the child lives and learns at his own pace without depending upon adults. The ground rules, didactic material, and other features of the prepared environment offer the framework for free activity and provide a dynamic balance between spontaneity and structure so needed by the learning-disabled child.

Most traditional educational practices have little actual scientific support. What is needed is a comprehensive educational methodology developed experimentally in the living laboratory of the prepared environment. Maria Montessori went far in this direction. Her approach, teamed with the latest educational technology, might well lead to the development of a truly scientific education for the learning-disabled child and for all children.

Montessori recognized that each child needs to work, that is, to master the challenge of interesting tasks. She also understood that children must be reasonably prepared before being expected to cope successfully with these tasks. By providing the learning-disabled child with preparation, the Montessori teacher can "teach success."

Likewise, children need to be allowed to finish things—to carry tasks through from beginning to end, and to repeat them as often as desired. Montessori spoke of the child's need to complete cycles of activity, and his "repetition of the exercises." Completing and repeating help develop the child's power of concentration, and for Montessori, concentration is the key to all teaching.

Although children learn through all their senses and have combinations of strengths and weaknesses in the sensory areas of vision, hearing, and touch, the traditional classroom has not provided sufficiently for these differences. Often, material to be learned is presented in only one manner to a whole group. In the Montessori prepared environment, a multisensory approach is employed, enabling each child to express his individual sensory preference and style of learning, helping, for example, the child who learns by doing or who through his own experience assimilates mathematics readily by manipulating concrete materials—rods, beads, and so on—and less readily through the spoken or printed word. Montessori sensorimotor education provides experience in comparing and classifying as a basis for further intellectual development. Learning-disabled children need, but generally do not receive, the orderly exposure to sensory stimuli afforded by the Montessori didactic material.

The Montessori "self-teaching" exercises and materials tap the learning-disabled child's interests and abilities during his formative years. They enable him to correct his errors and encourage the development of inner discipline by diminishing the need for teacher control. In brief, the freedom of the prepared environment permits the child to choose for himself and pace himself, while the "organization of work" inherent in the materials provides sufficient structure.

And what of the teacher for learning-disabled children? She will prepare the environment, take care of it, observe the children and discern and plan for their needs. A most important advantage of allowing the learning-disabled child to learn through direct contact with materials is the freeing of the teacher much of the time to observe how and what a particular child is learning. And responsibility for control of error is largely shifted from the teacher to the materials.

Maria Montessori spoke of the importance of spirit in teaching, reflected in the teacher's patience, humility, respect for the child, desire to observe, and willingness to diminish as the child expands. Most of her teaching is indirect. But she can and does take a more direct role when necessary. If the teacher is to be prepared to assume a basically new responsibility in education as a directress of human development, her preparation must reflect a new teacher education. Montessori teacher education provides a useful model.

The Montessori method of education has proved applicable to the needs of the learning-disabled child. Montessori herself began teaching youngsters with special needs over seventy years ago. The basic principles of Montessori theory emphasize the importance of knowing each child thoroughly and then tailoring the curriculum to meet his learning and emotional needs. Within the consistent and comforting structure of the classroom, the child is free to choose tasks, to move around, and to become independent. In this environment, most previously unsuccessful children learn and develop an improved self-concept.

Although Montessori is one answer for the learning-disabled child, it is not the whole answer. The regular Montessori environment must be simplified and made less distracting. For instance, class size should be limited to eight to twelve students.

It should be recognized that even with the best teaching and school environment, children will have lapses in learning and behavior. The road to success is not smooth. The Montessori materials can be the basis of the curriculum but should be supplemented with other materials designed for the learning-disabled child, as well as the textbooks he will meet when he returns to a regular class or school. The teacher must have training in special education and experience in teaching in a normal Montessori environment. Other professionals (psychologist, learning-disabilities specialist, speech therapist, and gross motor specialist) should be available for consultation or for work directly with the child.

The child with a learning disability can achieve his potential if he is provided special teaching to match his own pattern of needs. The authors believe the use of Montessori is one answer to the needs of the learning-disabled child.

Appendix A:

Selected Sources of Information on Children with Learning Disabilities

Aseltine School
4027 Normal Street
San Diego, Ca. 92103

Association for Children with Learning Disabilities
5225 Grace Street
Pittsburgh, Pa. 15236
(reprints and books available)

Council for Exceptional Children
Division for Children with Learning Disabilities
1920 Association Drive
Reston, Va. 22091

Learning Disability Program
Bureau of Education for the Handicapped
U.S. Office of Education
Washington, D.C. 20202

Optometric Extension Program Foundation, Inc.
Duncan, Okla. 73533
(a nonprofit, tax-exempt foundation for education and research in vision)

Marjorie Foster Coburn
Educational Consultant
5101 Overbrook Place
Colorado Springs, Colorado 80907

Albert D. Leary, Jr.
Executive Director
Leary School
7515 Lee Highway
Falls Church, Va. 22042

Marianne Frostig Center of Educational Therapy
5981 Venice Boulevard
Los Angeles, Calif. 90034

Academic Therapy Publications
1539 Fourth Street
San Rafael, Calif. 94901

The Journal of Learning Disabilities
5 North Wabash Avenue
Chicago, Ill. 60602

Other sources include: Education department
staff in your local college or university;
special education staff in your local public school
system; your state director of special education;
your local librarian.

Appendix B:

Selected Sources of Catalogs, Manuals, Films, and Materials Concerning Montessori, Learning Disabilities, and Special Education

American Guidance Service, Inc.
Publishers Building
Circle Pines, Minn. 55014

Christ Church Child Center
8011 Old Georgetown Road
Bethesda, Md. 20014
(*Target on Language*—teacher manual)

Developmental Learning Materials
7440 Natchez Avenue
Niles, Ill. 60648

Educators Publishing Service
Cambridge, Mass. 02138

Follet Materials Catalog
1010 West Washington Boulevard
Chicago, Ill. 60607

George Chyka Productions
P.O. Box 207
Alvin, Tex. 77511

Montessori Development Foundation
2108 Payne Avenue
Cleveland, Ohio 44114

Nienhius Montessori USA, Inc.
320 Pioneer Way
Mountain View, Calif. 94041

Practical Drawing Company
2205 Cockrell Avenue
Dallas, Tex. 75222

Preston—Special Materials for Children
71 Fifth Avenue
New York, N.Y. 10003

Sisters of Notre Dame
701 East Columbia Avenue
Cincinnati, Ohio 15215

Southwestern Montessori Training Center
P.O. Box 13466, North Texas Station
Denton, Tex. 76203

Special Education Materials, Inc.
484 South Broadway
Yonkers, N.Y. 10705
(Catalog 80—Learning Disabilities)

Appendix C:

Selected References to Montessori with Emphasis upon Learning Disabilities and Special Education

Argy, William, "Montessori Versus Orthodox: A Study to Determine the Relative Improvement of the Preschool Child with Brain Damage Trained by One of the Two Methods." *Rehabilitation Literature* 26, no. 10 (Oct. 1965): 294–304. The mean changes in developmental quotients favored the Montessori classes in the majority of cases.

Blackmore, Catherine, et al, "After Montessori: The First Grade; Part I." *Children's House* 7, no. 4 (Fall 1974): 18–20. A study of the adjustment to first grade of nineteen children with at least two years of Montessori. Findings included uniformly high reading performance.

Brutten, Milton, Richardson, Silvia O., and Mangel, Charles, *Something's Wrong with My Child*. New York: Harcourt Brace Jovanovich, 1973. A book written for parents about learning disabilities. Mentions Montessori as one useful technique for such children.

Edgington, Ruth, "Montessori and the Teacher of Children with Learning Disabilities: A Personal Odyssey," *Academic Therapy*

333332

Quarterly 5, no. 3 (Spring 1970): 219–21. The Montessori method is offered as a highly successful approach for learning-disabled children.

Evans, Ellis, *Contemporary Influences in Early Childhood Education*, 2nd ed. New York: Holt, Rinehart and Winston, 1975. An examination of trends in early childhood education for handicapped and normal children. The Montessori method is described, and research on the method is reviewed. The need for additional controlled research is noted.

Foster, Marjorie, "Montessori and the Learning Disabled Child." *Children's House*, 8, no. 1 (Summer 1975): 6–11. A Montessori resource-room approach for seven- to sixteen-year-old learning-disabled students is described.

Gitter, Lena, *The Montessori Way*. Seattle, Wash.: Special Child Publications, 1970. A practical guide to the Montessori essentials.

Gitter, Lena, *The Montessori Approach to Special Education*. Johnstown, Pa.: Mafex Associates, 1971.

Gordon, Ronnie, et al, "Performance of Neurologically Impaired Preschool Children with Educational Materials." *Exceptional Children* 38, no. 5 (Jan. 1972): 428–37. The Montessori cylindersSCB2* were one type of material used in this study.

Gotts, Ernest, compiler, *A Bibliography Related to Early Childhood Education, Child Development, and Preschool Handicapped Children*. Austin: Univ. of Texas, Dept. of Spec. Ed., 1971. Contains sources of Montessori information.

Guyer, Barbara, "The Montessori Approach for the Elementary-Age Learning Disabled Child." *Academic Therapy* 10, no. 2 (Winter 1974/75): 187–92. The Montessori language program is viewed as potentially helpful to the learning-disabled child because of its emphasis on developing an understanding of concepts or ideas through work with the child's hands with manipulable objects before the teaching of abstract solutions.

Heine, Lucy and Rahaim, Betty, *Prescriptive Education: Diagnosis and Implementation*. Marianna, Fla.: Jackson County Public Schools, 1973. Includes a brief review of Montessori materials in arithmetic.

Hellmuth, Jermone, ed., *The Special Child in Century 21*. Seattle, Wash.: Special Child Publications, 1964. Topics include adaptation of the Montessori method in developing visual perception in the special child.

Knight, Muriel, "Dyslexia to Autism: The Story of a Small Experiment." *Australian Children Limited* 5, no. 1 (April, 1975): 10–18. A speech therapist describes the Montessori-inspired treatment program she devised for her autistic patients with perceptual difficulties. She employs a concrete approach, with movable alphabets, and so on.

Kramer, Rita, "Maria Montessori, A Biography." New York: G. P. Putnam's Sons, 1976. A definitive biography presenting Maria Montessori as a woman and an innovative educator. Gives insight into her interest in exceptional children and the beginnings of her theories.

Mann, Lester, and Salvatino, David, eds. *The Second Review of Special Education.* Philadelphia: JSE Press, 1974. In this collection of eleven papers on current issues in special education is one by L. Goodman on the Montessori method with the handicapped, as well as a review of research on its validity.

Mann, Lynn, *A Performance Based Early Childhood-Special Education Teacher Preparation Program.* Monograph XIII—Social Development: Self-Help Skills. Charlottesville: Univ. of Virginia, School of Education, 1974. Includes, in a section on the relevancy of self-help skills, a discussion of the Montessori approach, which emphasizes practical life exercises. Various activities in Montessori to develop coordination and facilitate self-help skills are described.

Orem, R. C., *Montessori and the Special Child.* New York: G. P. Putnam's Sons, 1969. Montessori applications and techniques in special education; Montessori and Piaget: Montessori lectures on special education; her approach of using the child's senses and activity in learning.

Richardson, Sylvia, "A Pediatrician Looks at Montessori for Neurologically Impaired Children." *American Montessori Society Bulletin* 4, no. 4 (1966). Points out the value of the Montessori materials and techniques for the child who has a learning disability. Montessori's approach is seen as very compatible with a neurophysiological approach to learning.

Schramm, Barbara, *Case Studies of Two Down's Syndrome Children Functioning in a Montessori Environment: Research Project.*

Dayton, Ohio: Univ. of Dayton, School of Ed., 1974. The Montessori emphasis on sensorial activities and freedom of choice are seen as enhancing the retarded child's development.

Sciarra, Dorothy, and Dorsey, Anne, "Six year Follow-up Study of Montessori Education." *American Montessori Society Bulletin* 12, no. 4 (1974). In this study, a group of children who attended Montessori classes for at least four years, beginning during preschool, scored first of four groups in all seven of the Metropolitan Achievement Test subscores while they were in third grade.

Smith, Mortimer, et al, *A Consumer's Guide to Educational Innovations*. Washington, D.C.: Council for Basic Education, 1972. Includes an evaluation of the Montessori school as an instructional innovation.